The

Book

An Actor's Guide to Chicago

Compiled and Edited by
Kevin Heckman
Christine Gatto
Carrie L. Kaufman

Published by PerformINK Books, Ltd.

PerformInk Books, Ltd.
3223 N. Sheffield
Chicago, IL 60657

ISBN: 1-892296-00-4

Successor to "acting, modeling and dance," founding editors: Allyson Rice-Taylor, Emily Gerson-Saines

Editors' Notes

Welcome to our first edition of what we hope is the definitive guide to being a professional actor in Chicago. We have tried very hard to make this book useful to all actors, both the ones just coming to the city and the ones who have been here a while and know the score. We think that the breadth of our guide will enlighten even the most knowledgeable. At the very least, you can have a well-organized, quick reference guide at your fingertips.

We're already planning what we can do better in 1999. If you have any suggestions, please write us and let us know.

Just a word on how we've organized things. In alphabetizing the listings, we've placed individuals according to their last name, but businesses whose title includes a name by their first letter. For instance, Brian McConkey would be listed under M; but Brian McConkey Photography would be listed under B.

While our names are under the title, this book would have been quite nasty to publish had it not been for the wonderful staff at PerformInk. Managing editor Nicole Bernardi-Reis' editing expertise was well used. Listings editor Jessica Raab had many insights into actors' needs. Advertising manager Lisa Lu jumped in to make phone calls and help gather all the materials we needed. Most of all, we extend tremendous thanks to our designer Marty McNulty and our proof-reader Claire Kaplan. Your eyes would be hurting right now without them. We also want to thank the people who contributed their expertise in the form of articles, most notably Adrianne Duncan and PerformInk's kids-in-the-business expert Tina O'Brien.

We all hope this book saves you some time, informs you of some options, corrects some misinformation and generally makes it easier for you to focus less on the business and more on the art of acting. Break a leg!

Kevin Heckman
Christine Gatto
Carrie L. Kaufman

Table of Contents

Coming to Chicago

Moving to a new city can be a difficult task. Particularly in theatre, where networking is so important, arriving in a new place includes a ton of challenges. You've got to find an apartment, come up with some kind of income, register your car, and, not least, begin laying the groundwork for your theatrical pursuits.

All this can seem pretty overwhelming, so we've broken this chapter down into a step-by-step guide to settling yourself in Chicago. Even if you're not moving here, the apartment and neighborhood breakdown can be useful for any apartment hunter, and the unemployed will find some useful leads in the temporary agencies. For those of you who are moving here for the first time, allow us to say, "Welcome to Chicago!"

To Drive, or Not to Drive...

So shall you hear Of carnal, bloody and unnatural acts, Of accidental judgements, casual slaughters, Of deaths put on by cunning and forced caused, And in this upshot, purposes mistook.

Automobile:
n. **1.** a passenger vehicle for operation on ordinary roads, typically having four wheels and an internal-combustion gasoline engine.
-adj **2.** automotive

By Kevin Heckman

Complications

If you're **bringing a car to Chicago** from another state, you need to visit your local Illinois Secretary of State's office within 30 days to register your vehicle and obtain Illinois license plates. The cost is $13 for the title and $48 for plates. You must bring your title or loan agreement (if you haven't paid your car off) and out-of-state registration. To get an Illinois driver's license, you need your out-of-state driver's license, Social Security card, proof of your new Illinois address (a lease or a phone bill will suffice) and $10. For more information, call the Secretary of State's office at 312/793-1010. If you've owned your car for less than 3 months, you may have to pay Illinois sales tax before updating your registration. For information, call the Illinois Department of Revenue at 800/732-8866.

Next you'll have to visit the City of Chicago Department of Revenue. If you're moving into Chicago proper, you are supposed to have a **City Sticker**. The sticker does nothing for you, but a cop can ticket you for not having one if (s)he concludes you're a Chicago resident. This "wheel tax" costs $60 if you get it right away, and more if you don't. If your neighborhood requires a residential parking pass, you'll need a city sticker, no outstanding parking tickets and $10. Call 312/744-7409 for more information. Whew!

High insurance rates add to the financial burdens of car owners. Depending on what you're used to, your insurance cost could increase by as much as five times. Shop around, of course; some companies offer better rates than others, but prepare yourself to take a significant hit.

Driving in Chicago also offers certain challenges and difficulties. The streets lie in a straightforward grid, except for the occasional diagonal to throw you for a loop. It is also not uncommon for one way streets to conspire to keep you from heading in the direction you want. The actual pavement is filled with traps for the unwary driver. Potholes wider than your car punish both your alignment and your tires unmercifully. Of course the city crews are out there 24/7 fixing those very streets and making life easier for all of us. Or not. Many drivers see construction as a greater grief than the potholes, and the repairs, often temporary patches, don't always lead to a smooth ride.

The highway systems suffer from many problems as well. First, they are too small for the amount of traffic they handle. Long delays and rush hours that last from 6:30 - 9:30 in the morning and 3 - 7 at night result. At any time of any day it is possible to find yourself sitting in slowed traffic due to an accident, weather or the whim of the gods. Additionally, highway names can confuse outsiders. Residents don't refer to them by interstate numbers – only code names that don't appear on most maps. Needless to say, this makes translating a traffic report nearly impossible. Below is a highway map and a list of the main code names along with their actual designations:

Edens	I94 north of the I90/I94 merge
Kennedy	I90 north of the Loop, including the portion where I90 and I94 merge
Eisenhower	I290
Dan Ryan	I94 south of the Loop
Stevenson	I55
Tri-State	I294
Bishop-Ford	I94 south after it splits with I57
Skyway	I90 south of the Loop after I90 and I94 separate

Clear as a big opaque thing? Good!

Many of the interstates are actually tollways. Beware of automated, exact-change-only tolls. Not paying a toll carries a fine of up to $100 if you're caught.

Chicago is blessed with the second highest **gas prices** in the country after San Francisco. Whenever possible, buy gas in the suburbs.

The ultimate joy of driving in Chicago is the **Chicago driver.** Your compatriates on the roadways collaborate to make travel safe, quick and polite. Sadly not. If you've driven in different parts of the country, you may know that each region's drivers display unique on-road behavior. New York drivers are nothing like Texas drivers, for instance.

The Chicago driver, or *operatus obstinatus*, is a peculiar beast found congregating on Chicago streets and highways. They primarily feed on frustration caused by driving slowly in the passing lane. Other characteristics include willfully ignoring lane designations when passing, refusal to allow others of its kind to merge in heavy traffic and signs of torpor when driving in the rain.

Finally comes the end of a long day. You pull onto your home street, already thinking of hot tea, a book and your bed. Alas, one last task stands between you and these amenities: **Parking.**

Depending on where you are, this can be a Herculean endeavor. Some claim prayers to St. Martin, patron saint of parking, can cause spots to miraculously open before you. For the secular, there are other things to keep in mind. First, are you parking in a difficult area? Check the neighborhood guide in this chapter if you don't know. Second, watch for the signs announcing restricted parking during certain times. Every area is different in this respect. Watch out for street cleaning notices. In short, to avoid getting nailed with a big ol' ticket, read any and every sign on the street. Don't count on holidays exempting you from being ticketed. New Year's Day, Memorial Day, Independence Day, Labor Day, Thanksgiving and Christmas are all meter holidays, but cops may still ticket in residential parking areas.

If you are ticketed and you feel it was unfair, you can contest it by mail. Type up a polite letter explaining your side, include any supporting information and send it in. This does work, so if you think you're in the right, give it a try.

The Benefits

Convinced to go through life as a pedestrian? Wait! There are advantages to owning a car that, for some, make all the previously mentioned frustration worthwhile.

Chicago can be a difficult place to live for a pedestrian and owning a car can make day-to-day life much simpler. Try carrying a 50-pound bag of dog food on the eL, for instance. If you're not driving, get used to walking to the supermarket, the post office, etc.

Not just day-to-day life, but your theatrical life can be made simpler as well. Many suburban theatres are not near public transportation. Some theatres in the city require taking the train to a bus — a transfer that can add many minutes to your commute. Even theatres conveniently located near the eL often are surrounded by neighborhoods that get scary after dark. In all these situations, a car can be a blessing.

The eL, a capricious beast at the best of times, can turn a simple journey into a rerouted or delayed adventure. Usually Chicago public transportation is reliable, but the one time it's not is the one time you can't afford to be late.

Driving a car might actually save you money. The train is expensive, more so than parking your car sometimes. Some great day jobs require a car. Furthermore, owning a car makes certain neighborhoods accessible to live in, which can substantially lower your housing costs.

The greatest advantage to owning a car, though, is the flexibility it gives you as an actor. Being free to tell an agent, "Yes, I can be there in 20 minutes," may land you a job that might go to someone else while you're waiting for the eL.

It's a
Beautiful Day In
the Neighborhood

By Kevin Heckman

Chicago is a very simple city. It's laid out on a grid, with the exception of a few conveniently placed diagonal streets. All highways lead downtown, as do all train routes. A new arrival to the city will find it surprisingly easy to make one's way, whether driving or on foot.

Neighborhood:
n. **1.** A district or area with distinctive characteristics. **2.** a locality with reference to its character or inhabitants. **3.** A number of people living near one another.

Chicago is a very confusing city. The major highways are often referred to by their honorary names (Stevenson, Eisenhower, Edens) and not their numerical designations (55, 290, 90) which are more common on maps and street signs. If you ask Chicagoans where they live, they won't say Chicago, and they won't give the street. They'll say they live in Bucktown or Logan Square or Rogers Park. Public transportation, though conveniently color-coded, is referred to instead by its final stops. It's not the Red Line, it's the Howard-Dan Ryan.

Both of these paragraphs are true. Chicago is a simple city that seems to be full of strange codes to a newcomer. No one really knows where particular neighborhoods begin or end, or why it is that 94 West actually heads north. It may take a new arrival months to understand all of the names of the interstates and be able to make sense of a traffic report. What's a newcomer to do?

When it comes to neighborhoods, we can help. Neighborhood names are particularly useful to understand when apartment hunting, as most papers and realtors separate listings this way. Below is a breakdown of information on a selection of Chicago neighborhoods. Included are the boundaries (roughly), a small locator map and some idea of the parking, safety and accessibility by public transportation, rated from 1 (bad) to 5 (great). Finally, we've included quotes and observations from people who live there.

Neighborhood Breakdowns

Most of these breakdowns were compiled by talking with subscribers. **PerformInk** staffers also weighed in with their opinions. This doesn't make them gospel. Please remember these are the compiled thoughts of 2-7 people a neighborhood. This survey is completely unscientific, and should be taken as such. The best way to get a feel for a neighborhood is to go there and walk around.

Andersonville

Comments: *Residents cite the easy parking, affordable rents and great international restaurants in recommending Andersonville. It is home to many artists. In fact 21 percent of PerformInk's subscribers live there. Theatres in the neighborhood include Footsteps, Neo-Futurists and Griffin. There are also a number of actor hangouts: Simon's Tavern (where you can pick up a PerformInk), the Hop Leaf and Kopi, "a traveler's cafe." It also boasts the original Ann Sathers, which is the place for Sunday brunch and cinnamon rolls. The neighborhood is quite multi-cultural, with Swedish, Latino and Asian populations — and eateries. It also has a very big lesbian population. Women and Children First — a well-known feminist bookstore — has many special events with authors from around the country.*

Bounded by: Glenwood (1400 W.) Ravenswood (1800 W.) Foster (5200 N.) and Bryn Mawr (5600 N.)

Prices: Range from $500 for a one bedroom to about $325 a room for larger places.

Ratings: Public Transportation: 3.3
Parking: 4.2   Safety: 4.0

Buena Park

Comments: *This quiet neighborhood is "homey for being urban," says one resident. Some complain of the parking, but the neighborhood is praised by the many actors who live here. Many PerformInk subscribers live there.*

Bounded by: Marine Drive, Kenmore (1100 W.), Irving Park (4000 N.) and Montrose (4400 N.)

Prices: Range from $595 for a one bedroom to $450 a room for larger places.

Ratings: Public Transportation: 2.8
Parking: 3.7   Safety: 4.2

Bucktown

Comments: *Right off the expressway, this is a less accessible area by public transportation. A lot of small restaurants and bars are scattered throughout this area. It is quickly being gentrified and is often referred to in conjunction with its neighbor to the south, Wicker Park. There are a lot of filmmakers in Bucktown, many of whom can be found at a local tavern called The Charleston. It is yuppie artsy and quickly rising in price. Eclipse Theatre is in Bucktown, as is Trap Door.*

Bounded by: Kennedy Expressway, Western (2400 W.), North (1600 N.) and Fullerton (2400 N.)

Prices: Range from a studio for $400 to $600 a room for larger apartments.

Ratings: Public Transportation: 2.0
Parking: 4.0   Safety: 2.5

Edgewater

Comments: *This is a tough area to find parking, but public transportation is close. There's not much by way of shopping either. Many actors own their own places here. There is also a building called "Artists in Residence." The area can be dicey at night.*

Bounded by: Lake Michigan, Ravenswood (1800 W.), Foster (5200 N.) and Devon (6400 N.)

Prices: Range from a studio for $450 to $225 a room for larger places.

Ratings: Public Transportation: 3.3
Parking: 2.6   Safety: 2.5

Gold Coast

Comments: *This is a "great place to live" if you can afford it. Close to the lake with a lot of (very expensive) shops, "There's always a lot going on in the neighborhood." Again, many of the residents here own rather than rent, and the price for ownership runs in the millions, or at least the high six figures.*
This is the place, incidentally, where you can find Chicago's Magnificent Mile. It also boasts Mr. J's — one of the best hot dog stands in Chicago. It is very accessible to public transportation and within healthy walking distance of most agents' offices.

Bounded by: Lake Michigan, Clark, Oak (1000 N.) and North (1600 N.)

Prices: Range from a one bedroom for $1000 to $750 a room for larger places.

Ratings: Public Transportation: 4.0
Parking: 2.5   Safety: 4.4

Neighborhood Ratings:

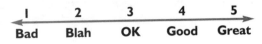

1	2	3	4	5
Bad	Blah	OK	Good	Great

Humboldt Park

Comments: *"There's a strong sense of community, lots of artists and lots of gangs," says one resident. Many PerformInk staffers live on the edges of Humboldt Park and feel that its bad reputation is quickly becoming undeserved. The park itself (part of the vast boulevard system designed to link all of Chicago's parks from the north to the south side) is*

Bounded by: Chicago (800 N.), Armitage (2000 N.), Western (2400 W.) and Pulaski (4000 W.)

Prices: Range widely from $400 for one bedroom to $200 to $400 a room for larger apartments.

Ratings: Public Transportation: 3.0
Parking: 4.0   Safety: 2.5

quite beautiful and safe to take children to during the day. It's one of the neighborhoods that is being hit by gentrification, but long-time residents — most of whom are Latino — are determined to not be priced out by development. As a result, strong multi-cultural ties have been formed and it is turning into a nice mix of people.

Hyde Park

Comments: *Centered around the University of Chicago, this is a college neighborhood tucked in the South Side. It's a very diverse area with a lot of bookstores and has the highest percentage of Nobel prize winners living in the city. Some great old buildings can be found there. If you're an architecture buff, it's definitely the*

Bounded by: Lake Michigan, 51st (5100 S.), Cottage Grove, and 60th (6000 S.)

Prices: Can be found around $300 - $400 a room for most apartments.

Ratings: Public Transportation: 2.0
Parking: 3.0   Safety: 3.0

place to be. Pockets can be quite safe; other areas are rather dicey. Court Theatre is in Hyde Park. The South Shore Cultural Center is close by.

Lakeview

Comments: *Lakeview ranges from very safe to kind of creepy depending on where you are. Parking is very difficult — especially at night. The only other complaint is that, while this is largely regarded as a great neighborhood, yuppification has begun in earnest. Frame houses have been torn down to make room for large brick and stone con-*

Bounded by: Diversey (2800 N.), Irving Park (4000 N.), Lake Michigan and the Chicago River

Prices: Range from a one-bedroom for $700 to $350-$600 a room for larger places.

Ratings: Public Transportation: 4.0
Parking: 2.0   Safety: 3.5

dos. **PerformInk's** *offices are in Lakeview (as of this printing), as are many theatres, including the Theatre Building, Bailiwick Repertory, Ivanhoe, Briar Street, Stage Left, the Organic/Touchstone, Shattered Globe, Turnaround, ImprovOlympic, About Face and many more. Actor hangouts include the L&L Tavern, Melrose Diner, The Gaslight and Bar San Miguel. It's a very post-college, young crowd with not too many families. Part of Lakeview is also known among the gay community as "Boys Town."*

Lincoln Park

Bounded by: North (1600 N.), Diversey (2800 N.), Lake Michigan and Clybourn

Prices: Range from a one bedroom for $1000 to $500+ a room for larger places.

Ratings: Public Transportation: 4.0
Parking: 1.5   Safety: 4.5

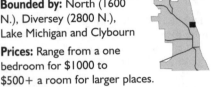

Comments: *Just south of Lakeview, this is a clearly upper-class neighborhood. Its residents enjoy a great deal of safety and convenience, although parking is very difficult. Lincoln Park was the up-and-coming neighborhood a decade ago and still boasts a lot of theatres. In fact, the Off-Loop theatre scene pretty much started in Lincoln Park (with a nod to Lakeview just to its north) in the 70's. Victory Gardens is located here in a building that once also housed the famed Body Politic Theatre. Steppenwolf and the Royal George also call it home. DePaul University makes for an interesting mix of theatre folk, yuppies and frat boys. John Barleycorn is one notable actor hangout, as is Sterch's. Then again, The Big Nasty is right next door to Sterch's. The Biograph (where John Herbert Dillinger was shot) is in this neighborhood. Act I Bookstore is on Lincoln next to the Apollo Theatre.*

Lincoln Square

Boundaries: Surrounding the corner of: Lincoln, Lawrence (4800 N.) and Western (2400 W.)

Prices: Range from $500 for a one bedroom to $250+ a room for larger places.

Ratings: Public Transportation: 2.5
Parking: 4.2   Safety: 3.8

Comments: *This neighborhood gets raves from its residents for the people and the community. It's less congested than the lakeside neighborhoods. A car is advantageous, but the eL does have a stop on Western and Lincoln, and there's a bus depot on Western. The buildings have a very Scandinavian feel, though the population is more a mix of White, Latino and Asian. Great Thai restaurants can be found in the area. There are also wonderful German bakeries. It's a nice quiet neighborhood with an old world feel.*

Logan Square

Bounded by: Fullerton (2400 N.), Diversey (2800 N.), Western (2400 W.), Central Park (3600 W.) and the Kennedy Expressway

Prices: Range from $200 - $450 a room.

Ratings: Public Transportation: 4.7
Parking: 5.0   Safety: 3.0

Comments: *Logan Square is one of the top areas for artists. In fact, artists moving into the neighborhood in the mid-80's helped to start the gentrification that has rapidly spread west and south. It's very community-based and multi-everything — race, culture, class. It is marked by large graystones and red brick flats. There are also some mansions that are still single family homes, especially in the Palmer Square area. There are some restaurants and bars that **Performlnk** staffers describe as "hip but neighborhoody." Abril Mexican restaurant is always crowded and is open until 4 a.m. on the weekends. The neighborhood is also marked by many churches and schools. Redmoon Theatre Company is located in the Logan Square area.*

Old Town

Comments: *"The area's great! It's eclectic, has theatres, bars, restaurants and it's convenient,"* says one subscriber. *Second City is in Old Town and, consequently, there are lots of actors' bars and hangouts, including The Last Act and Old Town Ale House. A Red*

Bounded by: Division (1200 N.), North (1600 N.), Clark (100 W.), Larrabee (600 W.) and Clybourn

Prices: Run about $750 for a one bedroom.

Ratings: Public Transportation: 4.0
Parking: 3.0   Safety: 4.0

Orchid Theatre is also in Old Town, as is Zanies comedy club. Pipers Alley movie theatre is in the same building that houses Second City. Parking is quite horrendous, unless you pay for it. Quite frankly, **PerformInk** *staffers can't quite figure out why most residents gave it a 3.0 rating. Old Town butts up against the Gold Coast and Lincoln Park, so it can be kind of pricey. On the other hand, it also butts up against Cabrini Green — a high-rise housing project that is nationally known for its safety problems.*

Pilsen

Comments: *Pilsen boasts a very large Mexican population and is home to the Mexican Fine Arts Museum. Decades ago, it was mostly Irish and Polish, and the remnants of those cultures can still be seen. It's currently going through gentrification, which is causing many political problems*

Bounded by: Roosevelt Road (1200 S.), Cermak (2200 S.), the Expressway and Damen (2000 W.)

Prices: Prices range from $350 for a one bedroom to $1000 for some rehabbed loft spaces.

Ratings: Public Transportation: 2.0
Parking: 4.5   Safety: 2.5

with long-time, mostly Latino residents. There are also lots of warehouses, which attract both theatre companies and developers. There is a very large artistic population, due to the low rents and large spaces. Blue Rider Theatre is on Halsted and 18th and has been there for over 10 years. Lookingglass Theatre had a rehearsal space in the area. The University of Illinois at Chicago (UIC) anchors the area to the south.

Printer's Row/ South Loop

Comments: *This area was a vast wasteland at the beginning of this decade, but rapid gentrification has made it one of the highest priced neighborhoods in Chicago. New construction overlooks the abandoned freight yards, which only seems to add a quaintness to the area. It helps that Mayor Daley moved from his boyhood*

Bounded by: Roosevelt Road (1200 S.) and 18th Street (1800 S.), the Lakefront and State Street (1W.)

Prices: Range from around $1,000 for a one bedroom loft to $1,500 and up for two or more bedrooms.

Ratings: Public Transportation: 3.5
Parking: 2.0   Safety: 3.0

neighborhood of Bridgeport (in the shadow of Comiskey Park) to this trendy area a few years ago, leaving traditionalists aghast. Transportation is quite good, with the eL running from the Loop just a mile or so to the north. Buses also are always on time. Parking isn't wonderful — unless you have a garage with your home or apartment, as many do. There are some nice restaurants in Printer's Row, but other than that it's very residential.

Ravenswood

Comments: *"Move here before the rents go up," says one resident. This affordable area is diverse and can be either quiet or noisy depending on where you are. It's pretty blue collar, with lots of single family homes. This is a neighborhood in which you will see kids playing in the yard or riding their bikes down the street. It's becoming yuppie and there is a growing gay population as Andersonville to the east becomes too expensive. Pauline's is a great breakfast restaurant, and don't miss Zephyr's for old-fashioned ice cream. The Ravenswood eL (or the Brown Line) ends in Ravenswood and numerous bus lines are always available.*

Bounded by: Clark, Sacramento (3000 W.), Montrose (4400 N.), and Foster (5200 N.)

Prices: Range from $450 for a one bedroom to as little as $235 a room for larger places.

Ratings: Public Transportation: 3.5
Parking: 3.3   Safety: 3.6

River West

Comments: *Large warehouses and loft spaces make up River West, which made it a prime target for revitalization in the late 80's and early 90's. After a fizzle in the area a few years ago, it is starting to live up to its potential. Chicago Dramatists Workshop is in River West, as is The Chicago Academy for the Arts — Chicago's answer to "Fame." Lots of good restaurants are popping up every day. There are a lot of filmmakers and companies in River West, more so than theatre artists. You definitely need a car in this area, and the closest grocery store is across the river in the Gold Coast. Safety is shaky depending on where you are and time of day.*

Bounded by: Grand (500 N.), Division (1200 N.), the Chicago River and the Kennedy Expressway

Prices: One bedrooms range from $600 to $750. Two bedrooms are around $850.

Ratings: Public Transportation: 1.0
Parking: 4.0   Safety: 2.5

Rogers Park

Comments: *This huge neighborhood forms Chicago's northern border. It's probably the most diverse of all the neighborhoods in Chicago. There are large Orthodox Jewish, Indian and Middle Eastern populations. Gay men moved up to condos in West Rogers Park in the early 90's. "It's a melting pot," says one resident. Diverse can describe the income ranges, too. Some areas are quite affluent, while others are very poor. Loyola University is in Rogers Park. Factory, Raven, Center and Lifeline are some of the theatres in this area. Don't take safety for granted. In some areas it's fine. In others — like on Howard street bordering Evanston — it's quite unsafe day or night.*

Rogers Park (East)
Bounded by: Lake Michigan, Ridge, Devon (6400 N.) and Howard (7600 N.)

Rogers Park (West)
Bounded by: Kedzie (3200 W.), Ridge, Devon (6400 N.) and Howard (7600 N.)

Prices: Range from $450 for a one bedroom to $300 a room for larger places.

Ratings: Public Transportation: 3.8
Parking: 2.3   Safety: 3.6

Roscoe Village

Comments: *This is a close-knit neighborhood, but residents will need to go elsewhere for their entertainment. It's definitely a place where "you can know your neighbors." The Damen is an actors' bar, as is the Village Tap. Higher Ground coffee shop also is quite popular. Lots of families and cheaper rents define the area, even now. Also, many Chicago filmmakers call this neighborhood home. It borders Lakeview to the east, so watch out for rising costs as people are priced out of Lakeview.*

Bounded by: Belmont (3200 N.), Addison (3600 N.), Lincoln and Western (2400 W.)

Prices: Range from $495 for a one bedroom to $300 a room for larger places.

Ratings: Public Transportation: 4.0

Parking: 4.0　　　Safety: 3.7

Saint Ben's

Comments: *This is a working class neighborhood that most residents feel is a "great place to live." One resident complained of the noise, but others praised the quiet feel, so it probably depends on where you are. It's just south of Ravenswood and has much of the same feel.*

Bounded by: Addison (3600 N.), Irving Park (4000 N.), Damen (2000 W.) and Western (2400 W.)

Prices: Runs about $400 for a one bedroom.

Ratings: Public Transportation: 3.3

Parking: 5.0　　　Safety: 4.4

Ukrainian Village

Comments: *This neighborhood lives up to its name and is not as diverse as many Chicago neighborhoods. The large Ukrainian population is augmented by artists who have flocked to the affordable housing. It's a very close-knit community. People watch out for one another. The Western Avenue border can be a bit dicey on the safety side, but it's generally pretty well-liked by the people there. Public transportation is not easy.*

Bounded by: Grand (500 N.), Division (1200 N.), Damen (2000 W.) and Western (2400 W.)

Prices: Two bedrooms run from $600 to $950. One bedrooms are $450 - $600.

Ratings: Public Transportation: 1.5

Parking: 4.0　　　Safety: 3.5

Neighborhood Ratings:

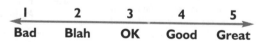

1	2	3	4	5
Bad	Blah	OK	Good	Great

Uptown

Comments: *Uptown is the once majestic area that has fallen into disrepair. The Aragon Ballroom still stands, though not as grandly as it did in the 20's and 30's. American filmmaking started in Uptown. Charlie Chaplin had a studio there before he went west. The famous Green Mill Lounge —* home of the Uptown Poetry Slam *— is in this area. Housing is very cheap — and for good reason. Safety is a major concern. Because it runs along the lake, people have been talking about this neighborhood coming up for some time, but it doesn't seem to be happening. Pegasus Players is in the area, as part of Truman College. The theatre is safe and quite nice, but people often complain about walking from their cars.*

Bounded by: Lake Michigan, Ashland (1600 W.), Irving Park (4000 N.) and Foster (5600 N.)

Prices: $450 - $650 for two bedroom

Ratings: Public Transportation: 3.5
Parking: 3.0   Safety: 1.0

Wicker Park

Comments: *Wicker Park is the neighborhood for any trendy artist in Chicago. If you want to be "in," you want to be in Wicker Park. Architecturally, it is defined by large Victorian mansions that were once grand and graceful and now have been cut up into apartments. There has also been a lot of rehab in the area over the past* few years, resulting sometimes in a strange mix of brand new brick and stone next door to an old Victorian. For all the rehab though, the area is still relatively inexpensive overall. This is the area where Nelson Algren lived and wrote, and the neighborhood is as tough and beautiful as an Algren book. Accessibility is somewhat of an issue, but not bad. The eL is the O'Hare line, which runs diagonally across the city to the airport. If you want to get up to Lakeview, where many theatres are, you have to go downtown first, then switch trains and head north. But buses do run regularly down North Avenue Ashland and Damen. Latino Chicago Theatre Company is in Wicker Park, reflecting much of the ethnicity of the neighborhood and nearby Humboldt Park.

Bounded by: Ashland (1600 W.), Western (2400 W.), Division (1200 N.) and North (1600 N.)

Prices: One bedrooms from $500 to $700. Two bedrooms from $750 to $1,000.

Ratings: Public Transportation: 2.5
Parking: 3.0   Safety: 3.0

Wrigleyville

Comments: *The home of the Cubs receives high praise from its residents, though parking can be difficult, particularly during baseball season. "I love it. I would recommend it to first-time Chicagoans. Easy access to bars and theatres,"* says one resident. Wrigleyville is home to young families and artists. It is not as expensive as Lakeview, it's neighbor to the south — unless, of course, you're in one of those buildings that overlooks the ballpark.

Bounded by: Halsted (300 W.), Clark, Addison (3600 N.) and Irving Park (4000 N.)

Prices: Range from $500 for one bedrooms to $400 a room for larger places.

Ratings: Public Transportation: 3.2
Parking: 2.6   Safety: 4.3

Evanston

Comments: *Evanston lies north of Chicago along the lake. Home to Northwestern University, this is a "down to earth, well-rounded community," says one resident. Evanston is mostly made up of* houses and mansions. *It can be quite exclusive, yet it can also be affordable around the university or west of the Ridge Street dividing line. Even so, living in Evanston is more expensive than living in Chicago. Taxes alone can be more than your mortgage pay-ment. The city has a bus system and also an eL line, which runs all the way down the lake to the Loop. Residents can go door-to-door from their apartment in Evanston to the Theatre Building in Lakeview in 20-30 minutes. Theatres include Fleetwood Jourdain, an African-American theatre, and the famed Piven Theatre Workshop. The city is expanding its commitment to the arts by building a new cultural center.*

Prices: $750 to $850 for one bedrooms. Two bedrooms run from $950 to $1,300.

Ratings: Public Transportation: 4.0
Parking: 4.5   Safety: 4.4

Oak Park

Comments: *This suburb lies just west of Chicago along the Eisenhower Expressway. "It's a diverse community, and we have a* lot of cultural things. Oak Park has a lot of actors. You'll always run into someone who's in the business," says a resident. Residents also cite the great schools and the supportive neighborhoods in recommending this suburb. Oak Park is a village and feels like one. Prices vary, but tend to be on the high side. Taxes are also a consideration here — the price for those wonderful schools and clean streets. Oak Park has a big gay population and is one of the few cities in the country that gives domestic partnership benefits to gay spouses of city employees. Theatres include Circle Theatre, Oak Park Village Players and the Oak Park Shakespeare Festival, which is a summer staple for actors and theatregoers.*

Prices: A larger apartment can be had for $500 a room.

Ratings: Public Transportation: 3.8
Parking: 3.8   Safety: 4.2

Skokie

Comments: *Skokie is more diverse and less expensive than its neighbor to the east, Evanston. While the suburb is largely thought of as the Jewish center of* the North Shore, the area has opened up to include many Asians and Latinos. Schools have a solid reputation, and there is an active park district. Convenient bus routes make it easy to reach the Howard eL stop in Evanston and many of the area's shopping and entertainment complexes. You can also take the "Skokie Swift," the one-stop extension of the eL that deposits riders at the Greyhound bus terminal. With the open-ing of The Northshore Center for the Performing Arts last year, Skokie is a big-time player on the theatre scene. Northlight Theatre is in the Northshore Center, along with the presenting company Center East.

Prices: $600 for one bedroom. Two bedrooms for $800 and up.

Ratings: Public Transportation: 3.8
Parking: 5   Safety: 4.8

Thanks to all **PerformInk** subscribers who took the time to answer our survey questions. Your contributions helped make this book possible. Much corroborating information was found on the Chicago Reader's Spacefinder at **www.chireader.com**

Finding an Apartment

C: Who builds stronger than a mason, a shipwright, or a carpenter?

O: Mass, I cannot tell.

C: When you are asked this question next, say "a grave-maker." The houses he makes last till doomsday.

Apartment:
n. **1.** a room or a combination of rooms for use as a dwelling. **2.** a building (apartment house) containing such rooms.

By Kevin Heckman

"I have to find an apartment."

These are dreaded words for many people, because what follows is... The Apartment Hunt! Maybe it's not quite *that* scary, but it's still not fun. However, following these easy steps can make it a little less painful.

STEP ONE - Talk to yourself

This step should not be done in public, but it is necessary. Before beginning the hunt, stop and consider a few things. What's your price range? How many bedrooms do you need? Are you living alone, or are roommates in your future? Do you have prospective roommates already, are you planning to find them once you have a place, or are you going to answer someone's ad seeking one?

Prepare a list of more specific questions. Carrying a checklist ensures no consideration will be left unanswered. For example:

Rooms: Where do you spend your time? How's the layout for privacy? How much does sound travel?

Parking: Check out the street days *and* nights. What are the local parking restrictions? Will you need a sticker?

Storage: Closets? Pantry? A secure basement?

Sound: Does the eL run nearby? Is there a heavily traveled street outside your window? Both of these will also make your apartment more dusty.

Natural Light: Which windows get light from where, when? Shaded windows make the apartment cooler in the summer. How early do you want the sun waking you up? Will it be in your eyes when you watch TV?

Security: Some say you can tell how safe a neighborhood is by the number of locks on the door. Maybe. Definitely worth noticing. Also, if it's a first floor or basement apartment, are there grills on the windows? How well lit is the street and entrance to the building? Again, check out the place at night to see how spooky it feels.

Pets: Not an issue for everyone, but are they allowed? If you have cats and the apartment has carpeting, be aware that a cat with claws will want to hurt the carpeting and your landlord probably will not appreciate it. If you have an outside type animal, is there a place to walk it?

Public Transportation: Is it accessible by train or bus? Does it have limited running times? How scary is it at night?

Neighborhood: Our neighborhood breakdowns can give you some of this information. Is there much crime? Who lives there? Families, college students, crack dealers? How accessible are stores, post office, etc.? Again, how is it at night?

Landlord: Who and where is your landlord? Does he or she live in the building? Is this his or her main profession or a sideline? Remember, this person has the capacity to make life great or horrid.

STEP TWO - Look

Fortunately, apartments are plentiful in Chicago. The most widely used source for leads is the *Reader*, a free paper that comes out Fridays. Their on-line apartment classifieds use a search engine that allows you to narrow your choices by zip code and cost (www.chireader.com). For the electronically minded, many apartment services have web sites as well. Apartment services, whether electronic or human, are usually free, but many smaller buildings don't get listed. If you're looking to sublease or be a roommate, check the call boards at Act I and the Equity office. Finally, walking around a neighborhood you like often yields possibilities that don't make it into the Reader.

Once you think you're interested in a place, be sure to visit it at different times. Remember, you'll be living there day and night.

STEP THREE - The Lease

Found an apartment? Great! All you have to do now is sign a lease. Your landlord-to-be will probably run a credit check on you. Mostly, (s)he'll be looking for evictions, bankruptcy and the like. Larger operations tend to be less flexible about bad credit. Some landlords will accept a larger-than-normal security deposit from a tenant in lieu of a good credit report.

STEP FOUR - Roommates (Optional)

Now that you've got a place, do you need roommates? Post notices at Act I Bookstore and the Equity office. Place a listing in the Reader and

PerformInk. Screen and ask for references. If you still need help getting
into the right frame of mind, go to your video store and rent *Shallow Grave*.

Roommate Services

Roommate Connection
160 E. Illinois #303
Chicago, IL 60611
312/755-1887

Special Housing

The following are non-traditional specialized housing. Call them for
more details.

Artists in Residence
6165 and 6161 N. Winthrop
Chicago, IL 60660
800/LIVE-ART
773/743-8900
773/743-8901 - fax

Eleanor Residence (women only)
1550 N. Dearborn Parkway
Chicago, IL 60610
312/664-8245
312/664-8062 - fax

Three Arts Club (for women)
(men - June, July, August only)
1300 N. Dearborn
Chicago, IL 60610
312/944-6250

Utilities

These fine institutions live to provide us with the basic necessities of
civilization. You'd never know it to deal with their customer service
departments, though. Ameritech, People's Gas, and ComEd all seem to
be competing for the crappy service on a stick award sometimes. All
you can do is keep track of who you talked to when and what they said.
Don't trust them. Always call to confirm.

Ameritech
800/244-4444

AT&T
800/222-0300

Commonwealth Edison
72 W. Adams, Chicago, IL 60603
800/334-7661

MCI
800/950-5555

Peoples Gas, Light & Coke Co.
130 E. Randolph, Chicago, IL 60601
312/240-4000

Sprint
800/877-7746

Workin'
Nine to Five

By Kevin Heckman

Sadly, most actors don't make a living. This may come as a shock, but it's true. The days of Humphrey Bogart becoming an actor because it pays better than producing are over. You will need a "real" job.

This job should pay you large sums of money, be interesting, enjoyable and let you take time off whenever you need it for auditions and shows. Good luck. Until you locate this mythical employment, you can always wait tables, temp or go full-time. Going full-time is the most secure, but usually the most restrictive. Many places who say they'll be flexible about auditions will turn out to have a problem the first time you ask to leave for a few hours. Temping and waitering both have pros and cons depending on your particular mental makeup.

If restaurants are your preference, there are hundreds to choose from. Ask around for places that are particularly good for performers. Also, check **PerformInk** classifieds for listings of other actor-friendly jobs.

Temporary Employment Agencies

A Personnel Commitment
208 S. LaSalle #189
Chicago, IL 60604-1003
312/251-5151
312/251-5154 - fax

Adecco Personnel Services
200 W. Madison #520
Chicago, IL 60606
312/372-6783
312/372-9732 - fax

AccuStaff, Inc.
401 S. Milwaukee #170
Wheeling, IL 60090
847/541-6220
847/541-6235 - fax

Advanced Personnel
Beth McDowell
1020 Milwaukee Ave. #105
Deerfield, IL 60015
847/520-9111
847/520-9489 - fax

Coming to Chicago

Appropriate Temporary Service
79 W. Monroe #819
Chicago, IL 60603
312/782-7215
312/704-4485
312/704-4195 - fax

ASI Temporaries
2 Illinois Center
233 N. Michigan #2306
Chicago, IL 60601
312/819-4695
312/819-4697 - fax

BPS Temporaries
200 N. LaSalle #1750
Chicago, IL 60601
312/920-6710
312/920-6744 - fax

City Staffing
2 N. LaSalle #630
Chicago, IL 60602
312/346-3400
312/346-5200 - fax

Dunhill of Chicago
68 E. Wacker Place -12th floor
Chicago, IL 60601
312/346-0933
312/346-0837 - fax

Loftus & O'Meara
166 E. Superior #410
Chicago, IL 60611
312/944-2102
312/944-7009 - fax

GREAT JOBS AT TOP COMPANIES.

We'll open doors of opportunity with temporary and full-time jobs that match your skills and ambitions. Call today and you could be working tomorrow.

312-372-6783

Adecco
THE EMPLOYMENT PEOPLE

Mack & Associates Personnel, Ltd.
Attn. Emilie Barta
100 N. LaSalle #2110
Chicago, IL 60602
312/368-0677
312/368-1868 - fax

Manpower Temporary Services
500 W. Madison #2950
Chicago, IL 60661
312/648-4555 • 312/648-0472 - fax

Norrell Temporary Services
35 E. Wacker Drive #620
Chicago, IL 60601
312/346-4470
312/444-9474 - fax

Paige Temporary, Inc.
5215 Old Orchard Road
Skokie, IL 60077
847/966-0111

Pro Staff Personnel Services
10 S. Wacker #2250
Chicago, IL 60606
312/641-6256
312/641-0224 - fax

Profile Temporary Service
222 N. LaSalle #450
Chicago, IL 60601
312/541-4141
312/541-1762 - fax

Right Employment Center
2275 Half Day Road
Banockburn, IL 60015
847/662-4646
847/914-0237 - fax

Select Staffing
208 S. LaSalle Street #1244
Chicago, IL 60604
312/849-2229 • 312/849-2234 - fax

Coming to Chicago

Seville Temporary Services
180 N. Michigan #707
Chicago, IL 60601
312/368-1272
312/368-0207 - fax

Staffing Consultants
Downtown:
55 E. Monroe, Mezz. level
Chicago, IL 60603
312/419-8849

Suburbs:
1701 E. Woodfield Road #903
Schaumburg, IL 60173
847/240-5300

TeleStaff Solutions
6133 N. River Road #720
Rosemont, IL 60018
847/318-8600

Temporary Professionals
Gloria J-N Piecha/Director
625 N. Michigan #600
Chicago, IL 60611
773/622-1202
773/622-1303 - fax

Personnel Services for trade shows, seminars and promotions. Models - Talent - Product Demonstrators - Samplers - Temporaries - Bi-Lingual Personnel - Put your personality to work!

Unique Office Services
360 N. Michigan Avenue #2001
Chicago, IL 60601
312/332-4183
312/332-2688 - fax

Building a Theatrical Network

Give thy thoughts no tongue. Nor any unproportioned thought his act. Be thou familiar, but by no means vulgar. Give every man thine ear, but few thy voice; This above all, to thine own self be true.

Networking:

n. **1.** an informal system whereby persons having common interests or concerns assist each other, as in the exchange of information or the development of professional contacts.

By Jessica Raab

Let's face it. It is who you know. Talent will only get you so far. This is depressing, but the case histories prove that many a no-talent yutz can make his/her way to fame and fortune by knowing the right people. To all those hard working and incredibly talented performers out there whining "It's not fair!," I offer my wonderful mother's words of wisdom: "Whoever said life was fair? Now shut up and get in the car."

Though networking is important, nothing is worse than being stuck in a conversation with a career schmoozer — the actor who calls just to "see what you're up to" and then feigns surprise when you tell him/her that you just began your internship with Jane Alderman Casting. The good news is there's a balance that can be struck in this business.

Lots of people sincerely like to talk about their work, and when you form a relationship not based entirely on your desperate desire to find work, you are networking successfully. Below is a list of things you may want to try in order to enlarge the number of people you know in Chicago and beyond.

1. A friend told me, before moving to Chicago, to **make a list** of absolutely everyone I knew here. This included people in and out of the business, relatives, friends, friends of relatives, relatives of friends, etc. I was pleasantly surprised to find I knew a lot of people before I even got here. I called many of them and found out all sorts of information about auditioning, classes, neighborhoods, restaurants, and so on. Most were enthusiastic about Chicago and excited to share their experience with me. Some never called me back. A tactful rule: call once, possibly twice. If they don't call you back, forget about it and don't take it personally. Some people like their privacy. Whatever you do, don't stalk them. That'd be bad.

2. More advice from my Mom: **If you want people to like you, ask them about themselves.** This goes hand in hand with number one, and is the reason why a lot of people did call me back. They love to talk about their experiences. It's very simple.

3. Take a class in something new. If you already have training, is there an aspect you want to work on? Taking a class is not only a great way to expand or refresh your skills, but you instantly meet a support group that understands what you are going through. Do some research before plunking down your money, and make sure the class is the right level for you. Your fellow students may have valuable insights on this business, so you not only want a quality instructor, but quality classmates.

4. Stay in touch with people. Some of my friends find it freakishly odd how many people I stay in touch with. Temping in an office is a terrific asset in terms of networking. Think about it: You are in a show, and as a temp every week you meet a new set of office buddies. You invite people with jobs to your show, they actually have the money to spend on a ticket, and they are thrilled to know someone in the show. A win-win situation. Make plans and send postcards. Return the favor; go see other people's shows and projects.

5. Be nice to everyone. Don't just blow sunshine up the butts of those people you think are important. In truth, everyone is important. The stage manager of today may be the casting director of tomorrow, but even if the stage manager of today is still the stage manager of tomorrow, be nice. Sandra Bullock is a star not only because she works hard, but because people really enjoy working with her. She's nice. Sean Young can't get arrested in Hollywood. Best Boys and Gaffers are usually directors-in-training. Your cab driver may run an award-winning theatre company. You just never know.

Training

Blood, Sweat and Acting Coaches

Professional dancers never stop taking class, so why should actors? Sure it cost money. Sure it takes a commitment of time. But it also keeps you sharp and ready for whatever may come up. Constant study and practice will give you the confidence you need when your agent calls you today for that big audition tomorrow.

Taking a class has other advantages, too. People get to know you. People get to see your work. Who knows what that will lead to when, for instance, one of your former classmates ends up directing a show.

Even if you can't afford the expense of a class, practice. Do scene-study with a friend. Learn to juggle. Every new skill you acquire is another reason for a director to cast you.

Learning
the art of acting

Speak the speech I pray you,
as I pronounced it to you,
trippingly on the tongue.

By Adrianne Duncan

The study of acting is one of the most rewarding and complex of the artistic disciplines. Unfortunately, it is also probably the most widely misunderstood. Since most of us already possess the basic tools needed to act — the ability to walk and talk, the ability to read, the ability to think — many believe that actors are just "playing themselves," that they are doing nothing more than reading the words on the page with a certain kind of expression.

Many of the achievements made in the study of acting in this century are also widely misunderstood. Terms like "motivation," "subtext" and "Method acting" have been derided as self-indulgent and deliberately esoteric processes. Who would criticize a violinist for playing scales, or a ballet dancer for working at the barre? And who would imagine that they could be a professional figure skater or pianist or painter without the years of training and practice necessary to master those disciplines? No one. It is obvious that no one could. However, when it comes to acting, many seem to feel that discipline and technique are not necessary, that actors are born with some sort of natural ability. And indeed many are. But there is a technique to this art form, and studying it will help you grow not only as an actor, but a person as well.

A Bit O' History

Acting as we know it today is vastly different than it was centuries ago. In the past, acting was mainly a declamatory and external exercise, with actors memorizing different types of gestures that were appropriate for certain emotions. With Stanislavski and the Moscow Art Theatre, things began to change. At the end of the 19th century, the Moscow Art Theatre and its director, Constantin Stanislavski, began to produce works by Anton Chekhov. These works, due to their intense naturalism and complexity, demanded a new style of acting — one that was not declamatory and artificial, but could truthfully show the real range of human emotion. This new style of acting relied on working from the inside out, on developing a "sense memory," on finding similarities between the actor's own life and that of the character in order to achieve the most perfect human truths on stage and be able to immerse oneself fully into that rich and complex imaginary, on-stage life. This was in direct contrast to the bombastic, external style of acting that directly preceded it.

Stanislavski's techniques would eventually be appropriated by Lee Strasberg and the famed Group Theatre. Without the formation of the Group, American and indeed modern acting as we know it might not exist. The Group Theatre was begun in the 1930's in the United States by a young group of actors and directors, most notably Strasberg, Elia Kazan, Cheryl Crawford and Harold Clurman (Clurman writes about the formation of the Group in his fascinating book, "The Fervent Years"). This group was dedicated to spawning a new, truer theatre based on Stanislavski's new ideas, one that showed life honestly through ensemble acting. The Group premiered such works as Clifford Odets' *Golden Boy* that shocked audiences with their realism and intensity.

After the Group stopped producing, many of its members and founders continued to teach. Many other teachers emerged after this era as well. They all immeasurably affected American acting style and the way it is taught today. Their names are legendary: Lee Strasberg, Stella Adler, Uta Hagen, Sanford Meisner, Viola Spolin and Michael Shurtleff. They all developed their own techniques and acting styles, all of which you can learn and draw from. Numerous books are published about each of these artists and their ideas which can complement your training greatly.

Developing Your Technique

The idea is to develop a technique that works for you. How you do it and where you do it is largely immaterial as long as you learn. If you have never taken an acting class in your life, but are burning to be cast in commercials, film or television, do not — I repeat, do not — go and take an on-camera or commercial class. Most trained actors can do commercial copy, as well as understand how to translate what they can do theatrically for the camera. It just doesn't seem to work as well the other way around. Seeing yourself on camera before you understand what you're doing can lead to self-conscious, manipulative acting and bad techniques that can take years to eradicate. Take a good, basic acting class first: one that gives you an idea of "who, what, where, when and why" on stage. Don't put the cart before the horse. At Northwestern, for example, freshman acting majors do not take acting class. They take theatre history, costume, lighting and set design; they run crew for shows. The idea is that you should know how a light is focused before you step into it. Sophomore acting students do not touch a script the entire first year. The emphasis instead is on freeing up the body, voice and perceptions through a variety of techniques. Junior acting majors do Greek tragedy first quarter, Shakespeare second quarter and Chekhov third quarter; it is only in senior year that students are able to touch contemporary scripts. The idea is to slowly build a foundation. To get back to the music analogy, you would not expect a musician to play a concerto without learning scales and arpeggios first. It would be impossible. Why would you view acting any differently?

Where to Go

There are several arenas in which an actor may study. Not everyone will have the opportunity to take advantage of all of them, but this short list will give you an idea of where to pursue your studies. Complete listings of the summer, undergraduate and graduate programs can be found in the "Directory of Theatre Training Programs" and the "Summer Theatre Directory," both published by Theatre Directories and available at Act One Bookstore in Chicago. All of the local acting programs and studios are listed in this book.

University Programs

At the undergraduate level, there are many excellent university training programs. Northwestern University and DePaul University are two such outstanding programs in the Chicago area. In my opinion, though, a theatre major should be a liberal arts concentration and not a conservatory degree. Actors graduating with theatre degrees should not do so at the expense of their broader education — that would be a disservice to themselves as people and as performers. If you have the opportunity to take advantage of an undergraduate program in theatre in addition to a liberal arts curriculum, it can provide an excellent base for you as an actor.

Summer Programs

Many institutions in the United States and abroad offer intensive summer acting programs. In England, the British-American Drama Academy (BADA) and the National Theatre offer programs of three to four weeks in length; the National Shakespeare Conservatory in upstate New York, Shakespeare & Company in Massachusetts and the American Conservatory Theatre in San Francisco, to name a few, also offer intensive summer training programs. Steppenwolf Theatre in Chicago will offer, beginning in the summer of 1998, a three-month-long program. The advantage of these types of programs is that you can receive a lot of training in a relatively short amount of time, often with top-notch instructors. The disadvantage? They are costly and time-consuming, with actors having to relocate and/or not work for a few weeks in order to participate.

Training locally

This is the area in which it may be most practical for many of you to study. Some of you may already hold undergraduate or graduate degrees; some of you may not have the opportunity to study full-time. In either case, there are excellent studios in Chicago that can provide you with terrific ongoing instruction, as well as keep you socially active with other performers. The areas in which you can study are extensive, from commercial and on-camera techniques at Act One Studios to cold reading at the Audition Studio. The Actor's Center teaches Meisner technique; Victory Gardens has many excellent classes, a great beginning acting class series among them. Second City has a training program for improvisation; you can study long-form improv techniques at ImprovOlympic. Familiarize yourself with who teaches what in Chicago. All the acting studios in the city are listed in this book. Ideally, you should be studying all the time. Just know that whatever your strengths or interests may be as an actor, it can always benefit you to study an area in which you have less experience or interest.

If you're just starting to study in Chicago without having had the benefit of a previous training or a long-term program, design one for yourself. Every actor should have a base. Start off with a few *basic* acting classes. Move on to monologues and scene study. Get used to working with other performers. Take a Meisner class. Take a cold reading class. Learn improv. Take a class at Shakespeare Repertory in Folio technique, which will open up a Shakespeare text to you in countless ways. Take an on-camera class. Take a commercial class. If you want total immersion, take Steven Ivcich's Professional Studio. But realize that you should probably study in a certain order, and not jump the gun before you're ready.

Graduate Programs

For those actors interested in taking their study of the craft to its highest level, studying at the graduate level may be appropriate. Realize, however, that the most prestigious programs are also the hardest to get into. These include Yale, New York University and Juilliard. There are other programs, many of which are associated with a regional theatre or university, that are also extremely difficult to get into. These include the American Repertory Theatre at Harvard, the American Conservatory Theatre in San Francisco and the Alabama Shakespeare Festival. You may audition for these and numerous other graduate programs either at each school during its audition season, or with the U/RTA (University/Resident Theatre Association) or the PTTP (Professional Theatre Training Program) when they come to Chicago. U/RTA and PTTP are consortiums of theatre training programs that have banded together and hold group auditions, generally in the spring of each year.

Turn to page 51 for a list of local Colleges and Universities offering M.F.A. degrees in theatre.

When most beginning actors get on stage with a script, they are lost. Without any technique, their only support is the script, and so they make the words everything. You need the *tools* to create reality on stage for yourself — otherwise the audience, whether it is for the Goodman, Voltaire or Empire Carpet, will never be able to believe you. You need to train. Besides, studying acting is fun. It is exhilarating, frustrating, mad-dening and exciting. It is psychology, literature and performance rolled into one. You can always learn. You can always get better. Every day you have new experiences that provide you with insight and understanding into not only yourself, but the characters you portray and, by extension, the world as well. Our craft *is* misunderstood. I think, then, it is up to us to be responsible to it if we choose to pursue it — to respect it and the others that choose it by recognizing it as a valid discipline.

Acting Classes

Act One Studios, Inc.
640 N. LaSalle #535
Chicago, IL 60610
312/787-9384
312/787-3234 - fax

Commercial Technique I - Get "camera-ready" for all types of commercial auditions.

Industrial Film & Ear Prompter - Learn to analyze and perform technical scripts and use an ear prompter.

TV & Film I, II & Workshop - Learn the "ins and outs" of the film and television world.

Fundamentals I, II & Intermediate Scene & Monologue Workshop - Learn to make effective choices from the script.

Acting Instinctively - Flexibility, creativity, and imaginative freedom are explored.

Meisner Technique I, II & Workshop - Leads to a very truthful moment-to-moment style of acting.

Monologue Workshop - Prepare two to four monologues for auditions.

Audition Technique I & II - Learn the art of the cold reading theatre audition.

Shakespeare Beg. & Adv. - Approaches based on the work of Shakespeare & Co.

Masters Class - An on-going scene study class taught by Steve Scott

Voice-Over I & II - Learn what it takes to be successful in the voice-over market.

Linklater I & II - Focuses on connecting the voice, breath, body and spoken language.

Actors' Center
3047 N. Lincoln #390
Chicago, IL 60657
773/549-3303

Technique (based on Meisner)
Monologues • Scene Study
Physical Character Work
Technique on Camera
TV/Film on Camera
Beginning Scene Study
Solo Performance

Auditioning Technique

Run by Director Kay Martinovich, the ACTORS' CENTER offers professional training for Chicago's working actors. Our instructors are professional actors, directors and movement specialists who are active in theatre, video and film. Our technique, based on the work and teachings of Sanford Meisner, aids actors in achieving real and truthful behavior on stage or in front of the camera. Our approach is geared toward seasoned actors continuing to develop their craft, as well as actors beginning a professional career.

Actors Gymnasium
Noyes Cultural Arts Center
927 Noyes St.
Evanston, IL 60201
847/328-2795

Circus Arts • Tap Dance • Stage Combat
Physical Comedy • Gymnastics
Mime • Juggling • Drum Performance
Contact Improvisation
Shakespeare Survival

Actors Workshop
1350 N. Wells #A300
Chicago, IL 60610
888/COLUCCI
312/337-6602
312/337-6604 - fax

Beginning Acting- On Camera
Advanced Acting- On Camera

Private Coaching: Ear Prompter, Monologue, Cold Reading, Commercial

Actors Workshop offers weekly ongoing classes for all levels. Each class starts with vocal warm-up, then commercials & scenes on-camera, which you can add to your demo reel. Call 1-888-COLUCCI to arrange a free visit and consultation with director Michael Colucci, author of VOCAL WORKOUT Booklet.

Audition Studio
20 W. Hubbard #2E
Chicago, IL 60610
312/527-4566
312/527-9085 - fax

Beginning Acting
Cold Reading II
Advanced Cold Reading
Monologue Workshop
Audition Strategies
Shakespeare
On-Camera I & II
Voiceover

Training is based upon the 12 Guideposts of Michael Shurtleff, well-known teacher, casting director and author of the actor's "bible," AUDITION. Mastery of these principles augments instinct and talent with a practical set of skills. This technique demystifies the actor's process and offers a path to creative discovery through action.

Blue Rider Theatre
1822 S. Halsted
Chicago, IL 60608
312/733-4668

Performance/ Composition for Actors and Non-Actors

Creativity Retreats for Women- Through the use of visual art and improv, women explore creative expression.

Creativity Workshop for Men- Similar to Creativity Retreats, but for men.

Borealis Theatre Company
P.O. Box 2443
Aurora, IL 60507
630/844-4928
630/844-5515

Chicago Actors Studio
1567 N. Milwaukee
Chicago, IL 60622
773/645-0222
773/645-0040 - fax

Acting as a Craft
Voice & Diction
Creating a Character
Scene Study
Shakespeare
Auditioning & Marketing
The Ear Prompter
Film, Commercial & Industrial Techniques
Making it in Trade Shows

CineFolio
916 S. Wabash #503
Chicago, IL 60605
312/409-8346

Free Associates
750 W. Wellington
Chicago, IL 60657
773/327-9917

Beginner I - Introduction to Unscripted Theatre
Beginner II - Ensemble Improvisation
Intermediate I - Creating Unscripted Theatre
Intermediate II - Performing Styles
Advanced I - The Big Picture
Advanced II - Performance Workshop
Acting for Improvisers
Brush Up Your Improvisational Shakespeare
Creating An Original Character

Illinois Theatre Center
400A Lakewood Blvd
Park Forest, IL 60466
708/481-3510

708/481-3693 - fax

Beginning Acting- Technique, Scene Study
Advanced Acting

ImprovOlympic
3541 N. Clark
Chicago, IL 60657
773/880-9993

ImprovOlympic provides Chicago's most comprehensive training in long-form improvisation. Students learn several long-forms, including The Harold. Students are regularly selected from our

Training Center to perform in the ImprovOlympic Cabaret, and all students who complete the program develop and appear in a long-form show directed by improv guru-in-residence, Del Close.

International Performance Studio
1517 W. Fullerton
Chicago, IL 60614

KV Studios
1243 N. Damen
Chicago, IL 60622
773/907-1551

Technique
Scene Study
Monologue
Commercial Copy
Shakespeare
Audition
Actors' Support Group

Neo-Futurists
5153 N. Ashland
Chicago, IL 60640
773/275-5255
773/878-4557 - fax

Performance Workshop
Advanced Performance Workshop– both classes are studies in performance art.

Piven Theatre Workshop
927 Noyes #102
Evanston, IL 60201
847/866-6597
847/866-6614 - fax

Scene Study: Intermediate to Professional
Theatre Games

Improv & Scene Study

Monologue Preparation

Players Workshop of Second City
2936 N. Southport
Chicago, IL 60657
773/929-6288
773/477-8022 - fax

Creativity through improvisational techniques is the foundation of our training program. Whether performing a role on stage or just preparing for one, our six term program teaches how to tap into strenghts and weaknesses, and make these skills work in stage performances, auditions, commercials and in life itself.

Porchlight Theatre
1019 W. Webster
Chicago, IL 60614
773/325-9884

Rachael Patterson Audition Studio
20 W. Hubbard #2E
Chicago, IL 60610
312/527-4566

Private Coaching

Sarantos Studios
2857 N. Halsted
Chicago, IL 60657
773/528-7114
773/528-7153

Second City
1616 N. Wells
Chicago, IL 60614
312/664-3959
312/664-9837 -fax

Steven Ivcich Studio
The Professional Studio
1836 W. North Ave
Chicago, IL 60622
773/235-9131

Professional Studio Program - 40 weeks of intensive training

Taste of the Professional Studio - 4 week survey of the above

Actors Workspace - 4 to 8 week classes

Theatre on the Lake
Chicago, IL
312/747-0820

Training Center for Actors, Directors, Playwrights & Singers
1346 W. Devon
Chicago, IL 60660
773/508-0200
773/508-9584 - fax

Professional Classes for beginning to advanced levels:

Technique

Scene Study

Monologues

Camera Technique

Playwrighting

Directing

Advanced Characterization

Audition Intensive

Shakespeare

Vocal Performance - Singing

Training Center
for Actors, Directors, Playwrights & Singers
Professional Classes:
Beginning thru Advanced Programs
"Serious training for the Serious Artist."
Call (773)508-0200 ACT NOW!

Trap Door Theater
1655 W. Cortland
Chicago, IL 60647
773/384-0494
773/384-2874 - fax

Victory Gardens Theatre
2257 N. Lincoln
Chicago, IL 60614
773/549-5788
773/871-3000
773/549-2779 - fax

Acting I

Basic Acting

Monologues

Musical Theater

Literary Adaptation

Performing Shakespeare

Scene Study

Speech & Movement

The Stage Actor On Camera

The Victory Gardens Training Center is the educational arm of our theatre. Our eight-week sessions are taught by local professionals and are designed to serve both the beginner and the working profes-sional. For more information or a brochure, please call 773/549-5788 and ask for Darcy or Andre.

Voices, Inc.
241 Douglass Way
Bolingbrook, IL 60440
800/385-5375
630/739-0044
630/739-3837 - fax

Voice-Overs – Is it for You?
Voice-Over: Copy Interpretation

Wisconsin Theater Game Center
2397 Lime Kiln Rd.
Baileys Harbor, WI 54202
920/854-5072

Dance Classes

Key: B - Ballet   J - Jazz   M - Modern   T - Tap

Academy of Classical Dance of India
620 Ridgewood Court
Oak Brook, IL 60521
773/296-1061

Classical Indian Dance

Academy of Movement and Music
605 Lake Street
Oak Park, IL 60302
708/848-2329
708/848-2391 - fax

B - J - M - Creative Movement - Spanish

American Dance Center Ballet Company
10464 W. 163rd Place
Orland Park, IL 60462
708/747-4969
708/747-0424 - fax

B - J - M - T - Ballroom

Art Linkletter's Young World
1263 S. Main Street
Lombard, IL 60148
630/627-4412

B - J - T - Acrobat - Lyrical

Ballet Arts Studio of Wilmette
729 Lake Avenue
Wilmette, IL 60091
847/256-6614
847/256-5318 - fax

B - Flamenco

Ballet Chicago
185 N. Wabash #2305
Chicago, IL 60601
312/251-8833

B

Belle Plaine Studio
2014 W. Belle Plaine
Chicago, IL 60618
773/935-1890
773/935-1909 - fax

B - J - T

Betsy Herskind School of Ballet
2740 W. Touhy Avenue
Chicago, IL 60645
773/973-6446

B - J - T

Beverly Art Center
2153 W. 111th Street
Chicago, IL 60643
773/445-3838

B - J - M - T

Boitsov Classical Ballet
410 S. Michigan #300
Chicago, IL 60605
312/663-0844

B: Vaganova Technique, Moscow Bolshoi Theatre System of Training.

Boulevard Arts Center
6011 S. Justine
Chicago, IL 60636
773/476-4900

B - M - T - African

Chicago Human Rhythm Project
1319 W. Granville #2
Chicago, IL 60660
773/761-4889

T

Chicago Moving Company
3035 N. Hoyne
Chicago , IL 60618
773/880-5402
773/880-5402 - fax

M - Aerobic Jazz - Creative Movement -
Special Populations

Chicago Multicultural Dance
Center/Bryant Ballet
806 S. Plymouth Court #G4
Chicago, IL 60605
312/461-0030
312/461-1184 - fax
B

Chicago National Association of
Dance Masters
5301 E. State Street #301
Rockford, IL 61108
815/397-6052
815/229-6080 - fax

B - J - M - T

Conservatory of Dance
10339 S. Pulaski Road
Chicago, IL 60655
773/239-2042

B - M

Teresa Cullen
729 Lake Avenue
Wilmette, IL 60091
847/256-6614
847/256-5318 - fax

B - Flamenco

Dance Academy
5721 W. Irving Park Road
Chicago, IL 60634
312/527-9606

B - J - T - Hip Hop - Swing
Beginning to Advanced

Dance Center Evanston
610 Davis
Evanston, IL 60201
847/328-6683
847/328-6656 - fax

B - J - M - T

Dance Center
of Columbia College
4730 N. Sheridan Road
Chicago, IL 60640
773/989-3310
773/271-7046 - fax

B - J - M - T - African - Musical Theatre -
Composition

Dance Dimensions
595B N. Pinecrest Road
Bolingbrook, IL 60440
630/739-1195

B - J - T - Ballroom - Pointe - Tumbling

Dance Therapy Center
Fine Arts Building
410 S. Michigan
Chicago, IL 60605
312/461-9826

B - M
Private: B - M - Ballroom

Dance Center North
540 N. Milwaukee
Libertyville, IL 60048
847/367-7970
847/367-7905 - fax

B - J - T - Urban Jazz

Domenick Danza
5116 N. Glenwood
Chicago, IL 60640
773/728-7305

Musical Theatre

**Diana's Dance
and Fitness Dynamics**
Diana Duda
429 Park Drive
Glenwood, IL 60425
708/755-8292

B - J - T

*Musical Theatre, Choreography, Ballroom
Beginning to Intermediate*

Discovery Center
2940 N. Lincoln
Chicago, IL 60657
773/348-8120

B - J - T - Ballroom - Ethnic - Social Dance

Barbara Dubosq
847/831-3383

B - T

Emergence Dance Theatre
804 1/2 Market
P.O. Box 186
DeKalb, IL 60115
815/758-6613

B - T - Middle Eastern Dance

**Evanston School of Ballet
Foundation**
1933 Central Street - 1st floor
Evanston, IL 60201
847/475-9225

B

Folk Dance Council of Chicago
914 Horne Street
St. Charles, IL 60174
630/232-0242

Folk Dances from around the world

Golden's School of Dance
1825 W. Golf
Schaumburg, IL 60194
847/885-8511

B - J - T - Ballroom

Gus Giordano Dance Center
614 Davis
Evanston, IL 60201
847/866-9442
847/866-9228 - fax

B - J - M - T - Hip-Hop

Hedwig Dances
2936 N. Southport #210
(Administrative Offices)
Chicago, IL 60657
773/871-0872
773/296-0968 - fax

*Contemporary and World Dance - Latin -
African - Physical Theatre Lab*

Jo's Footwork Studio
Chris Fagan
1500 Walker
Western Springs, IL 60558
708/246-6878

B - J - M - T

Joel Hall Dance Center
934 W. North Avenue
Chicago, IL 60622
312/587-1122
312/587-0568 - fax

B - J - M - T - African - Egyptian

**Judith Svalander School of
Ballet**
83 E. Woodstock Street
Crystal Lake, IL 60014
815/455-2055

B

Training

Kast & Company Liturgical Dancers
5320 S. University
Chicago, IL 60615
773/643-8916
Private: M - Sacred Dance

Lou Conte Dance Studio
1147 W. Jackson
Chicago, IL 60607
312/461-0892

B - J - M - T - Hip-Hop

Mayfair Academy of Fine Art
1025 E. 79th
Chicago, IL 60619
773/846-8180

Milwaukee Ballet
504 W. National Avenue
Milwaukee, WI 53204
414/643-7677
414/649-4066 - fax

B

Phil Moss
822 Westwood Lane
Wilmette, IL 60091
312/507-7729
847/251-2771 - fax

Israeli Folk Dance

Muntu Dance Theatre of Chicago
6800 S. Wentworth #3E96
Chicago, IL 60621
773/602-1135
773/602-1134 - fax

African Dance

Najwa Dance Corps
1900 W. Van Buren #0505
Chicago, IL 60612
312/850-7224
312/850-7141

J - M - T - African - Carribean

Outabounds Performance Company
3319 W. Berwyn
Chicago, IL 60625
773/463-3956

Improvisation

Patterson School of Ballroom Dance
1240 Sunset Road
Winnetka, IL 60093
847/501-2523

Ballroom Dance

Rockford Dance Company
711 N. Main
Rockford, IL 61103
815/963-3341
815/963-3541 - fax

B - M - Ballroom

Royal Scottish Country Dance Society
Ree Grisham
3550 N. Lakeshore Drive #227
Chicago, IL 60657
773/528-7824

Ruth Page Foundation
School of Dance
1016 N. Dearborn Parkway
Chicago, IL 60610
312/337-6543

B - J - T

Sammy Dyer School of Theatre
2411 S. Michigan Avenue
Chicago, IL 60616
312/842-5934

School of Performing Arts
200 E. 5th Avenue #132
Naperville, IL 60563
630/717-6622

J - T

**Shelley's School
of Dance and Modeling, Ltd.**
450 Peterson Road
Libertyville, IL 60048
847/816-1711

B - J - M - T - Hip-Hop - Pointe

Barbara Silverman
Chicago, IL
773/267-3363

Emily Stein
Chicago, IL
773/868-9723

B - M - Pointe - History

Studio Two Dance Arts, Ltd.
1014 Weiland Road
Buffalo Grove, IL 60089
847/808-0987

B - J - M - T - Hip-Hop

Talent Forum
450 Peterson Road
Libertyville, IL 60048
847/816-1711

B - J - M - T

Tango 21
Jorge Niedas
Chicago, IL
888/TANGO21
312/688-1319 - pgr.

B - Tango

Teresa y los Preferidos
729 Lake Avenue
Wilmette, IL 60091
847/256-6614

B - Flamenco

Stage Combat Classes

R & D Choreography
7443 N. Hoyne #1N
Chicago, IL 60645
773/743-7436

Modeling Classes

Chicago Model Productions
2208 Midwest Road
Oakbrook, IL 60521
630/571-1122

Model Image Center
1218 W. Belmont
Chicago, IL 60657
773/348-9349

The Models Workshop
118 W. Kinzie Street
Chicago, IL 60610-4508
312/527-2807

John Robert Powers
27 E. Monroe #200
Chicago, IL 60603
312/726-1404
312/726-8019 - fax

Scriptwriting Classes

Chicago Alliance for Playwrights
1225 W. Belmont
Chicago, IL 60657
773/929-7367
773/338-3036
773/327-1404 - fax

Chicago Dramatists Workshop
1105 W. Chicago
Chicago, IL 60622
312/633-0630
312/633-0610 - fax

Dedicated to producing new works and developing new plays, as well as developing the skills of playwrights.

Training Center for Actors, Directors, Playwrights & Singers
1346 W. Devon
Chicago, IL 60660
773/508-0200
773/508-9584 - fax

Turn to page 88 for help with finding talent and casting agents.

Acting Coaches

Dawn Arnold
312/327-1572

Bud Beyer
1979 S. Campus Drive
Evanston, IL 60208
847/491-3372

Belinda Bremner
Chicago, IL 60614
773/871-3710

An audition is a job interview using someone else's words. The key to a successful audition is finding an author who tells your story in your words. Your choice of audition material speaks volumes. Decide what that message is and then craft your audition.

Courtney Brown
1902 W. Addison
Chicago, IL 60613
773/878-3865

Dexter Bullard
773/227-6487

Dexter Bullard is a Jefferson-Cited director with 10 years experience in casting and has taught acting and audition technique for over four years at University of Illinois, Columbia College, Actors' Center, and Audition Studio. Gain immediate results for auditions or breakthroughs in acting over a few sessions. Very affordable sliding scale.

Michael Halberstam
Riders Theatre
c/o Books on Vernon
Glencoe, IL 60022
847/835-5398

Shakespeare Seminar

Lori Klinka
916 Rainbow Drive
Glenwood, IL 60425
708/709-0880
708/709-0881 - fax

Lori has taught acting for 15 years. She helps people focus their careers, including: goal setting, information about agents, headshots, finding auditions, etc. Lori is a private coach for technique in commercials, industrials, film, monologues and ear prompter for ages 10 and up.

Ruth Landis, Inc.
5054 N. Hamlin
Chicago, IL 60625
773/463-3780
773/463-3683 - fax

A mind-body-spirit holistic approach to acting for theatre (monologues, scenes, cold reading), on-camera, and voice-over, striving to make auditioning and artistry a joyous experience, focusing on personal empowerment and relief of performance anxiety. Ruth has taught at Northwestern, Columbia College and Roosevelt University, Victory Gardens and privately for over 15 years. $60.00 per hour.

Bob Mohler
5431 N. Wayne
Chicago, IL 60640
773/907-0674
773/275-6473

Kurt Naebig
711 S. Norbury
Lombard, IL 60148
630/495-7125
312/527-4566

Kathryn Nash
Chicago, IL
312/943-0167

*Acting - Voice - Speech Coach
Member - AEA, AFTRA, VASTA (Voice and Speech Trainers Assoication)*

Private instruction specializing in:
-Vocal techniques for stage and voiceovers
-Standard American diction
-Dialect acquisition and reduction
-Monologue coaching to integrate "kinesthetic, vocal and emotional modes" within the acting process. Call 312/943-0167.

John Robert Powers
27 E. Monroe #200
Chicago, IL 60603
312/726-1404
312/726-8019 - fax

Raven Theatre
6931 N. Clark
Chicago, IL 60626
773/338-2177

Malcolm Rothman
3900 N. Lake Shore Drive #12E
Chicago, IL 60613
773/281-4686

I provide intensive on-camera training and career guidance for experienced stage actors interested in getting into film, TV and commercials. AEA- AFTRA- SAG actor with 20 years experience in Chicago and L.A. markets. Proven technique as taught by Amy Sunshine. No beginners. No contracts. No B.S.

Scanlon Swanbeck Studio
Nancy Scanlon, John Swanbeck
3354 N. Paulina #206
Chicago, IL 60657
773/281-5321

Career Consultation. Coaching: Film/TV, monologues, commercials, voice-over - demo producing. Nancy was a Film/TV Agent at Harrise Davidson and later ran the Voice-over Dept. at Geddes Agency. Both direct theatre, film, industrials and produce voice-overs. John is slated to direct an independent film produced by and starring Kevin Spacey.

Training

Fredric Stone
5040 N. Marine Drive #3A
Chicago, IL 60640
773/334-4196

Fredric Stone, a working professional actor/director with over 25 years experience (New York and Chicago), coaches actors in monologue preparation for auditions - both contemporary and classical. He created and taught The Audition Workshop at Organic Theatre and currently teaches an 8-week Performing Shakespeare class at Victory Gardens Theatre.

Find out what else you need for auditions in The Actor's Tools starting on page 53.

Karen Vaccaro
1243 N. Damen
Chicago, IL 60622
773/907-1551

"The moment you lose yourself on stage marks the departure from truly living your part and the beginning of exaggerated false acting." — Stanislavski

I can't say it any better than this. Together we create a space that is both disciplined and nurturing. From the beginner to the working actor, you'll get the tools and the coaching needed to move your work and your career forward with grace and ease. Credits include: Broadway, Off-Broadway, Steppenwolf, Goodman, Television, Film.

VoiceWorks
3817 N. Bell
Chicago, IL 60618
773/528-5905

Voice-Over Coaches

Audio One, Inc.
Kirk Johnson
325 W. Huron #512
Chicago, IL 60610
312/337-5111
312/337-5125 - fax

Bosco Productions
661 W. Lake Street
Chicago, IL 60661
312/466-9900
312/466-0201 - fax

Charles Fuller
800/385-5375
630/739-3837 - fax

Long-time voice-over talent, I teach detailed 8-week courses on the subject at Columbia 2. For information, please phone 312-3344-5269. The full course is supported by the textbook "The Business of Voiceovers," 270 pages. Detailed, accurate, and professional, this textbook will get you started. Fax credit card orders to 630/739-3837, include name as on card, expiration date, and card number, or mail check or MO for $19.95 plus $3 S&H to VOICES, 596 N. Pinecrest Road, Bolingbrook, IL 60440.

Sound Advice
Kate McClanaghan
2028 W. Potomac #2
Chicago, IL 60622
773/772-9539
773/772-9006 - fax

VoiceOver 101
Ray Van Steen
325 W. Huron #512
Chicago, IL 60610
312/587-1010
312/337-5125 - fax

Private, individual coaching sessions in voicing TV/Radio commercials. Record-playback method in recording studio environment, basics through full production of voice demo tape. Ray Van Steen is a working voice-over professional, published writer on the subject and has voiced thousands of commercials. Phone for free, no obligation brochure: 312/587-1010.

Voice-Over U
Sherri Berger
Chicago, IL
773/774-9559
773/774-9555 - fax

Voice-Over Workshop
1943 W. Belle Plaine Avenue
Chicago, IL 60613
773/528-7041

Dialect Coaches

Martin Aistrope
1243 N. Damen #2
Chicago, IL 60622
773/276-4665

Belinda Bremner
Chicago, IL 60614
773/871-3710

Voice/Speech Coaches

Marina Gilman
5701 S. Dorchester
Chicago, IL 60637
773/955-0016

Marina Gilman is a certified Feldenkrais® Practitioner who holds a M.M. in voice and M.A. in Speech and Language Pathology. She specializes in prevention and rehabilitation of voice professionals including singers, actors, and broadcast journalists. Her approach to teaching is a combination of somatic education and traditional voice training.

Kathryn Nash
Chicago, IL
312/943-0167

Acting- Voice- Speech Coach Member- AEA, AFTRA, VASTA (Voice and Speech Trainers Assoiciation)

Private instruction specializing in:

-Vocal techniques for stage and voice-overs

-Standard American diction

-Dialect acquisition and reduction

-Monologue coaching to integrate "kinesthetic, vocal and emotional modes" within the acting process. Call 312/943-0167.

Cecilie O'Reilly
2023 N. Damen
Chicago, IL 60647
773/486-3649

Rak Vocal & Healing Clinic
6056 W. Irving Park Road
Chicago, IL 60634
773/283-8349

Dr. Mark Rose, Ph. D.
1922 W. Montrose @ Puppet Parlor
Chicago, IL 60613
773/275-1202

Ann Wakefield
1500 N. LaSalle #3C
Chicago, IL 60610
312/751-9348

William Rush Voice Consultants
410 S. Michigan #528
Chicago, IL 60604
312/360-1039
630/620-1270

Frank Winkler
1765 George Court
Glenview, IL 60025
847/729-1893

Singing Coaches

Tamara Anderson
1023 Barberry Lane
Round Lake Beach, IL 60073
847/546-5548
847/546-5717 - fax

*Tamara has taught hundreds of students from recording/touring professionals to beginners. With over 25 years of experience in pop, rock, blues and country performance and recording, including voice-*over and jingles, she has a true working knowledge of how to keep the voice and mind healthy while getting the most out of your performance.*

Boulevard Arts Center
6011 S. Justine
Chicago, IL 60636
773/476-4900

Mark Burnell
2008C W. Potomac
Chicago, IL 60622
773/862-2665
773/862-2665 - fax

The Center For Voice
410 S. Michigan #635
Chicago, IL 60605
312/360-1111

A non-profit arts organization promoting singing through education and performance. Private lessons for all styles. Call for brochure.

Ron Combs
917 Castlewood Terrace
Chicago, IL 60640
773/271-8425

David H. Edelfelt
1243 W. Foster
Chicago, IL 60640
773/878-SING

Through the use of solid vocal technique and unique coaching skills, I will guide you toward doing anything you wish with your voice, whether in Musical Theatre, Classical, Cabaret, Jazz or Pop. I aim to enable you to allow every decision you make regarding your singing to be one of artistic choice, and not of technical or emotional limitation.

Marina Gilman
5701 S. Dorchester
Chicago, IL 60637
773/955-0016

Marina Gilman is a certified Feldenkrais® Practitioner who holds a M.M. in voice and M.A. in Speech and Language Pathology. She specializes in prevention and rehabilitation of voice professionals including singers, actors, and broadcast journalists. Her approach to teaching is a combination of somatic education and traditional voice training.

Patricia Martinez
4072 N. Sheridan #3D
Chicago, IL 60613
773/549-1073

Cecilie O'Reilly
2023 N. Damen
Chicago, IL 60647
773/486-3649

Dr. Mark Rose, Ph. D.
1922 W. Montrose @ Puppet Parlor
Chicago, IL 60613
773/275-1202

What a Voice Productions (The Vocal Studio)
Karyn Sarring
P.O. Box 577227
Chicago, IL 60657
773/769-6480
773/989-0033 - fax

Vocal Technique, Physiology/Health of the Voice, Performance Coaching, Vocal Pedagogy, Audition Preparation, Career Counseling, Ear Training, Music Reading and Theory.

Patrick Sinozich
916 W. Belle Plaine
Chicago, IL 60613
773/528-4440

Peggy Smith-Skarry
1347 W. Winona
Chicago, IL 60640
773/728-5240

The Voice Works
Ruth Allyn
Near North
Chicago, IL 60610
312/944-3867

William Rush Voice Consultants	Frank Winkler
410 S. Michigan #528	1765 George Court
Chicago, IL 60604	Glenview, IL 60025
312/360-1039 • 630/620-1270	**847/729-1893**

Instrument Coaches

Sherwood Conservatory of Music
1014 S. Michigan Avenue
Chicago, IL 60605
312/427-6267

Movement Coaches

Courtney Brown	Robin Lakes
1902 W. Addison	1979 S. Campus Drive
Chicago, IL 60613	Evanston, IL 60208
773/878-3865	**847/491-3147**

Kevin Rechner
2142 W. Concord Place
Chicago, IL 60647
773/862-5804

Soaring Movement Workshops
2970 N. Sheridan Road #1021
Chicago, IL 60657
312/409-4714
773/327-1572

Learn the "loaded language" of movement for actors and discover your body's expressive potential while accessing your creativity at the same time! Soaring Workshops are offered regularly by Dawn Arnold and The Moving Dock Theatre Company. Workshops can also be arranged for your group. Call 312/409-4714 or 773/327-1572 for information.

T. Daniel Movement Theatre Company
1047 Gage Street
Winnetka, IL 60093
847/446-0183

Movement Classes, specifically Mime, all levels.

Speech Disorders

Center for Stuttering Therapy
1570 Oak Avenue
Evanston, IL 60201
847/864-8289

Krause Speech & Language Services
233 E. Erie #815
Chicago, IL 60611

312/943-1927
312/943-2692 - fax

Bonnie Smith
1855 W. Taylor
Chicago, IL 60612
312/996-6520
312/996-1282 - fax

Universities - Local

The following are nearby universities offering M.F.A. degrees in theatre.

Central Michigan University
Steve Berglund- Area Coordinator of Theatre and Interpretation
Central Theatre Office
333 Moore Hall
Mt Pleasant, MI 48859
517/774-3961
517/774-2498 - fax

Central Missouri State University
Dr. Ed See- Chairman, Theatre Dept.
Martin 113

Warrensburg, MO 64093
660/543-4020
660/543-8006 - fax

Columbia College
72 E. 11th
Chicago, IL 60605
312/663-1600
312/663-9591 - fax

Training

DePaul University - Theatre School
2135 N. Kenmore
Chicago, IL 60614
773/325-7929
773/325-7920 - fax

Eastern Illinois University
600 Lincoln Avenue
Charleston, IL 61920
217/581-3110
217/581-6027 - fax

Eastern Michigan University
103 Quirk
Ypsilanti, MI 48197
313/487-1220 • 313/487-3443 - fax

Illinois State University
Department of Theatre
Normal, IL 61790-5700
309/438-8783
309/438-7214 - fax

Indiana University
Dept. of Theatre & Drama
Bloomington, IN 47405
812/855-4503
812/855-4704 - fax

Michigan State University
Department of Theatre
149 Auditorium
East Lansing, MI 48824
517/355-1855
517/355-1698 - fax

Northern Illinois University
Department of Theatre Arts
DeKalb, IL 60115
815/753-1335
815/753-8415 - fax

Northwestern University
1979 S. Campus Drive
Evanston, IL 60208
847/491-3170
847/467-2019 - fax

Purdue University - Lafayette
1376 Stewart Center G77A
West Lafayette, IN 47907-1376
765/494-3074
765/496-1766 - fax

University of Illinois - Chicago
1040 W. Harrison (M/C255)
Chicago, IL 60607-7130
312/996-5286
312/413-0421 - fax

University of Iowa
Dept. of Theatre Arts
107 Theatre Building
Iowa City, IA 52242
319/335-2700
319/335-3568 - fax

University of Michigan-Ann Arbor
Department of Theatre & Drama
2550 Frieze Building
Ann Arbor, MI 48109-1285
734/764-5350
734/647-2297 - fax

University of Wisconsin
821 University Avenue
Madison, WI 53706
608/263-2329
608/263-2463 - fax

Wayne State University
Department of Theatre
4841 Cass Avenue #3225
Detroit, MI 48202-3489
313/577-3508
313/577-0935 - fax

Western Illinois University
Department of Theatre
101 Browne Hall
Macomb, IL 61455
309/298-1543
309/298-2695 - fax

The Actor's Tools

There are so many things the actor needs. Beepers, photographs, sheet music, etc. They're your investment in your business. If you don't have lots of money, plan strategically. Don't rush out and buy everything all at once. Get what you need most at the time you need it. Budget the items you do need in on over a period of months. Also, shop around. Make sure that you're getting the best quality for the best price.

Following are some places to start your search. For those new to the business, this chapter can serve as an introduction to the tools of the acting trade.

JOHN Cascarano

John Cascarano Photography
319 N. Western Ave. Chicago Il 60612
312-733-1212

A picture's worth $1,000 Bucks

Look here upon this picture,
and on this,
The counterfeit presentment
of two brothers.

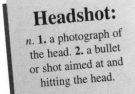

Headshot:
n. **1.** a photograph of the head. **2.** a bullet or shot aimed at and hitting the head.

By Adrianne Duncan

The Headshot

No professional actor in Chicago should be without a good, **professional headshot**. A headshot is an 8" x 10" black-and-white photograph of yourself. A good quality headshot is probably the best investment you can make in your career as an actor. You simply cannot work without one. Not only is your headshot your business card, but a good one can open doors for you and, for print work, you can often be booked from your headshot alone.

Conversely, a bad headshot can close doors for you. In the acting industry, there are many more actors than jobs, and there are many more actors who have good headshots than agencies have room for. So if you have a mediocre headshot, you may be setting yourself up for failure.

In the initial stages of your career, your headshot precedes most personal contacts you make. If it's a bad one, you may never get to that second stage. Don't fool yourself into thinking that getting a cheaper, lower quality headshot to start out with is a smart move. It isn't. If you're not yet at that stage where you consider yourself professional and trained enough to invest in top-of-the-line pictures, then do not invest in any. You will inevitably make bad impressions and lose money in the long run.

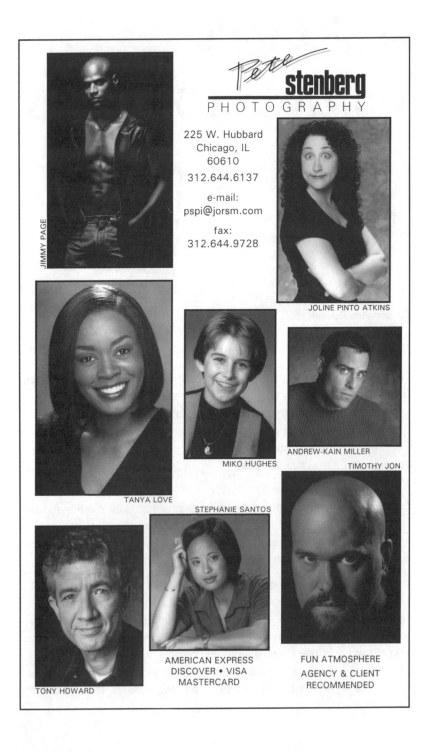

JIMMY PAGE

Pete stenberg
PHOTOGRAPHY

225 W. Hubbard
Chicago, IL
60610

312.644.6137

e-mail:
pspi@jorsm.com

fax:
312.644.9728

JOLINE PINTO ATKINS

TANYA LOVE

MIKO HUGHES

ANDREW-KAIN MILLER

TIMOTHY JON

STEPHANIE SANTOS

TONY HOWARD

AMERICAN EXPRESS
DISCOVER • VISA
MASTERCARD

FUN ATMOSPHERE
AGENCY & CLIENT
RECOMMENDED

Of course, there are exceptions to every rule; you may have a friend studying photography who happens to get an amazing shot of you. Fabulous. But most of us should play it safe and stick with established, experienced photographers who will charge rates in accordance with their ability.

The Photographer

Finding the right headshot photographer for you requires a bit of **research.** First, you must find out who they are. Not all photographers can do theatrical portraiture (a fancy name for headshots). It is not the same as fashion photography or standard portraiture. **Read PerformInk** and pay attention to the ads, look in the Photographers section of this book and talk to your friends. Act One Studios has a portfolio of different headshot photographers' work that you can browse through.

Once you come up with three photographers that you are interested in, make an appointment with each of them for a **consultation.** Reputable headshot photographers will give you a free consultation, which will give you a chance to see their work and get a feel for them and their studio. Are you comfortable with them? Do you feel comfortable in the space? If you don't like the photographer, your pictures will suffer. Pick someone who you like personally as much as you like their work. You should also hire a **professional makeup artist** to be present at the session. This will set you back another $75-$100, but it is vital. The camera in black-and-white photography can see only light and shadow. Makeup for that medium is all about contour and is nothing like regular street or even stage makeup. Men may even want to have a makeup artist present to help with hair and even out skin tone.

The actor's headshot is a specific kind of thing. It has nothing to do with fashion or modeling, in which the idea is often to convey an attitude or an image. The only thing the headshot is selling is you. It is a portrait of you — not you portraying a role or a fantasy of you — but you. **It has to look like you and it has to feel like you.** The headshot comes from the inside. Your eyes are probably the most important thing in a headshot and should convey something. They can convey a multitude of things, but it has to be something and preferably something *specific*. The most interesting headshots are the ones in which it looks like the subject is thinking something. You have to project a feeling, and make sure that feeling comes through to the viewer.

The Actor's Tools

The Session

Once you've chosen your photographer, you need to prepare for the **session.** What you wear should be basically what is always in your clothes hamper — the clothes that you wear most often and feel best in. Clothing should show your shape, whatever it is, but should not be overly tight or revealing. You need to show that you have a waist. For a more commercial shot, you should look like you would look on a good day — not necessarily dressed for a business interview, but groomed. Watch TV and get ideas from commercials and shows you can see yourself in. You do need to have some marketing savvy about what image you want to project.

Ask your photographer if they have a tape player or a CD player and bring music that you love — it will help you relax and project a specific mood. Get a good night's sleep before your shoot, eat a good breakfast, drink lots of water, and relax! Trust your photographer and your intuition.

After your session, your photographer will give you a set of **proof sheets** to pick out your pictures. Whatever you do, don't let your mother pick your headshot! This work is for qualified professionals only and should not be attempted at home. If you have an agent or agents, drop off your proof sheets for them to look at. If you have experienced actor friends, let them look at your proof sheets. You do need a lupe to look at proof sheets — an eyepiece which will magnify your proofs eight times their size and is available at most photography stores. Hang on to your proof sheets for a week or two before you choose which ones you want blown up. See which shots people are gravitating toward. They may not necessarily be the ones you like. If you need to, have several shots blown up. Pictures can look a little different once you see them at their actual size. Pick two or three pictures to be duplicated. One should be commercial and one should be film and theatre — the other could be something specific, like industrial or sitcom. The pictures should all have a distinctly different feel and look to them. Pay attention to the composition of your pictures as well. Pick shots that are interesting and pleasing to the eye.

The Processing

After you decide on your two or three shots, you need to get them duplicated. There are several excellent **reproduction houses** listed in this book. You need to decide on the style of your pictures. Matte finishes with a border are currently in vogue in Chicago; ask your photographer

and your agent for their judgment. Many reproduction houses will tell you that the font (the type style for your name, which is generally printed on the bottom of the picture) doesn't matter. I think it does. A font can be creative and express you. If you have access to a computer and can print out your own name with your chosen font, do it. It'll also save you money when you get your pictures duplicated. Pay attention to the type of paper. You can use litho paper, which is about five times as cheap as photographic quality paper but takes the quality of the picture down a few notches and tends to get brownish over time. Spend the money. For photo postcards, I recommend that photographic quality paper also is used; however, some people complain that it's hard to write on or run photo paper through a printer. Use your judgment.

Photographers

Linda Balhorn
201 N. Wells #410
Chicago, IL 60606
312/263-3513
312/236-8870 - fax

Basil Fairbanks Studio
Noel Grigalunus / Cordelia Westcott
4908 N. Glenwood
Chicago, IL 60640
773/907-9567
773/907-0050 - fax

...people on location...people in the studio... whatever your need...this is the number to call
BASIL FAIRBANKS
STUDIO, INC.
773.907.9567

Brad Baskin
850 N. Milwaukee
Chicago, IL 60622
312/733-2192

Becht Photography
676 N. LaSalle - 601
Chicago, IL 60610
312/642-5408 • 312/337-5040 - fax

Whether you are looking for images that are straightforward, or style's leading edge, I will work with you in a comfortable and relaxed atmosphere to capture the look you desire. Appointments are available to suit your schedule, including evenings/weekends. Becht Photography is conveniently located in Chicago's River North.

Bianco Scotti Productions
2001 W. Pershing - 5th floor
Chicago, IL 60609
312/301-9373

Blair Holmes Photography
3841 N. Oakley Ave.
Chicago, IL 60618
773/604-8543
773/583-8979 - fax

BLAIR PHOTOS
Need a Great Headshot?
Want to *Own* Your Negatives?
Great Rates! Instant Service!
(773) 604-8543

Scott Chambers
2701 W. Grand
Chicago, IL 60612
312/850-0263

**Chris VandeGuchte
Photography**
3157 S. Archer #2R
Chicago, IL 60608
773/847-0777
773/847-0007 - fax

Christopher Jacobs Studio
1443 W. Grand Avenue
Chicago, IL 60622
312/563-0987
312/563-0588 - fax

Martin Christopher
801 S. Plymouth #311
Chicago, IL 60605
312/987-9067

Classic Photography, Inc.
John Karl Breun
Box 1023
Wheeling, IL 60090
847/808-8373

David Puffer Studio
847/733-1300

David Renar Studio
2023 W. Carroll Avenue
Chicago, IL 60612
312/226-0001

*RENAR is Chicago's complete publicity
source! We offer a range of services from
outstanding professional photography to
computerized enhancement/retouching
and more! So whether you've just started
or are a seasoned pro, RENAR is the
place to call! For more information, or to
schedule a FREE consultation, give us a
call or view our online portfolio at
http://www.renar.com!*

Debbie Leavitt Photography
2029 W. Armitage
Chicago, IL 60647
773/235-6777

Josh Dreyfuss
312/987-1892

Englehard Studio
1278 N. Milwaukee
Chicago, IL 60622
312/235-4596

Dale Fahey
773/973-5757

Tom Fezzy
1163 E. Ogden Avenue
Naperville, IL 60565
630/548-3650
630/548-9764 - fax

Foto Rio
1248 W. Eddy #3
Chicago, IL 60657
773/244-1003
312/599-1670 - pgr.
773/529-3298 - fax

Ken Frantz
415 W. Huron - 2nd floor
Chicago, IL 60610
312/951-1077

Furla Photography & Video
1440 Waukegan Road
Glenview, IL 60025
847/724-1200

G. Thomas Ward Photography
1949 W. Leland #1
Chicago, IL 60640
773/271-6813

The Actor's Tools

Gerald Peskin Photography, Inc.
715 Vernon Avenue
Glencoe, IL 60022
847/835-3360

Jennifer Girard
1455 W. Roscoe
Chicago, IL 60657
773/929-3730
773/871-7762
773/871-2308 - fax

*"A HEADSHOT DOESN'T HAVE TO BE
BEAUTIFUL, IT HAS TO BE TRUE
. . .THEN IT'S BEAUTIFUL!"*
*Headshot and 3/4 shots prices: 3 rolls
(36 exp. per roll), proof sheets and 4
8x10 custom prints done in my lab for
$285 or 1 roll (36 exp), proof sheet and 2
8x10's for $165. Shoot in studio or loca-
tion. 2 day proof turn around.*

Jennifer Girard, Jr.
3428 N. Janssen
Chicago, IL 60657
773/929-2625
773/929-2620 - fax

Guy Cardarelli Photography
119 W. Hubbard - 3rd floor
Chicago, IL 60610
312/321-0694

Image Shop
33 Hoyt Place
Aurora, IL 60506-4131
630/859-0004
630/859-0026 - fax

Images by Onate
3500 Midwest Road, Oak Brook, IL
630/655-2212
708/496-0961

Dale Fahey
PHOTOGRAPHER

◆ HAIR
◆ MAKE-UP
◆ WARDROBE

Greg Brown   Gauri Ramnath   Darrell Stokes

773◆973◆5757

Gary Jochim
1651 W. Fulton #2
Chicago, IL 60612
312/738-3204 • 312/738-3204 - fax

Joel DeGrand Photography
600 W. Van Buren #905
Chicago, IL 60607
312/258-1178 • 312/258-1176 - fax

John Cascarano Photography
319 N. Western, Chicago, IL 60612
312/733-1212 • 312/733-2715 - fax

Joseph Amenta Photography
555 W. Madison #3802
Chicago, IL 60661
773/248-2488

Kenneth Simmons Photography
3026 E. 80th Street, Chicago, IL 60617
773/684-7232

Jean Krettler
6410 N. Glenwood #1S
Chicago, IL 60626
773/274-5545

L.A. Lyte Studios
1255 S. Wabash
Chicago, IL 60605
312/922-5983
312/922-5159 - fax

L.L. Rice Photography
Chicago, IL
773/404-9269

Quality professional headshots, composites and portfolios for aspiring and/or working models, actors and dancers. Our creative approach achieves unique images in our convenient Northside studio located only 15 minutes from the loop. Over 17 years experience photographing models. Call today for prices and an appointment.

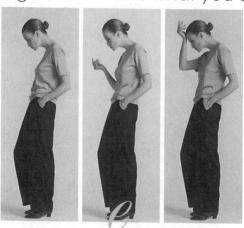

unforgettable. that's what you are.

edda taylor photographie
courthouse square, suite 304   crown point, in 46307   **219.662.9500**

Larry Lapidus
2650 W. Belden #304
Chicago, IL 60647
773/235-3333 • 773/278-9714 - fax

*My directorial technique sets me apart
from other photographers. The rapport we
develop is the most essential tool for capturing your true individuality. We will
express your character in a fashion that is
perfect for commercial purposes in theatre,
television or film. Photographic fees:
$375.00, including 45 minute consultation,
three rolls, and two 8 x 10 custom prints.*

John Marciniak
820 W. Lake #202
Chicago, IL 60607
800/690-2096

Brian McConkey
312 N. May #6J
Chicago, IL 60607
312/563-1357
312/563-1516 - fax

Michael Brosilow Photography
1370 N. Milwaukee
Chicago, IL 60622
773/235-4696

Michael Scarpelli Photography
3136 Maple Avenue
Berwyn, IL 60402
800/560-7100

Moore Photographic
773/276-0249

Cristin Nestor
Chicago, IL 60640
312/988-0452

Joshua Owens
8240 N. Harding
Skokie, IL 60076
847/673-9446
312/851-3118

Papadakis Photography
17 Lexington Road
South Barrington, IL 60010
847/428-4400
847/428-4403 - fax

Specializing in people photography, especially *children*. We shoot ads, hire talent and help connect talent with agents. We work with *all* 40 agents and casting directors. We have helped talent go on to shoot print ads, commercials, pilots, TV and feature films. Call for a *free* marketability evaluation!

Patrick Harold Productions, Inc.
1757 W. Augusta Boulevard
Chicago, IL 60622
312/226-3831
312/226-3832 - fax

The Actor's Tools

Paul Sherman Photography
213 N. Morgan #3F
Chicago, IL 60607
312/633-0848

Payton Studios
Reginald Payton
118 W. Kinzie - 2nd floor
Chicago, IL 60610
312/661-0049

Pete Stenberg Photography
225 W. Hubbard - 6th floor
Chicago, IL 60610
312/644-6137
312/644-9728 - fax

Capturing you at your best! Specializing in headshot photography for actors and composite photography for models, both children and adults - 20 years of experi-ence- Agency recommended - Free con-sultation - Makeup artist on staff - Credit cards accepted - Any questions? Please call! Let us help you take the first step in

opening the doors to your career! e-mail: pspi@jorsm.com

Peter Bosy Photography
222 S. Morgan #4D
Chicago, IL 60607
312/243-9220
312/243-9255 - fax

Photography by Dennis
3636 N. Marshfield
Chicago, IL 60613
773/404-8021
773/281-6811 - fax

Photography by Mary Clare
1201 Laura Lane
Lake Bluff, IL 60044
847/680-3686

Photography by Mike Canale
614 Davis Street
Evanston, IL 60201
847/864-0146

$129.00 Headshots. Satisfaction guaranteed. Located in the Giordano Dance Center, one block from CTA & Metra stops. Established 1980.

Quantity Photo
Rich Pace
119 W. Hubbard 2nd floor
Chicago, IL 60610
312/644-8290 • 312/644-8299 - fax

Here at Quantity Photo, we've been helping acotrs, models, and entertainters for over 50 years. Our owner-manager, Rich Pace, alumni of Second City, brings his expertise to personally help you and oversee the pro-

duction of your photos. Our hallmarks are Quality, Friendly Service and Low Prices!

Robert Erving Potter III
2056 W. Superior Street
Chicago, IL 60612
312/226-2060 • 312/226-1918 - fax

Rubinic Photography
1049 N. Paulina
Chicago, IL 60622
773/489-2929
773/477-4141 - fax

Suzanne Plunkett Photography
3047 N. Lincoln #300
Chicago, IL 60657
773/477-3775

Gary Trantafil
312 N. May #100
Chicago, IL 60607
312/666-1029

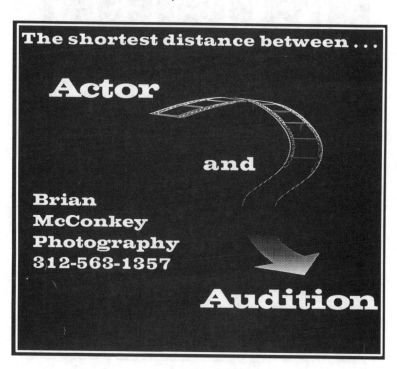
The Actor's Tools

Triangle Studio
3443 N. Broadway
Chicago, IL 60657
773/472-1015
773/472-2201 - fax

Steven Wright
1545 N. Larrabee
Chicago, IL 60610
312/943-1718

Photographic Reproductions

A&B Photography
650 W. Lake Street - 2nd floor
Chicago, IL 60661
312/454-4554 • 312/454-1630 - fax

Artisan Printing & Lithography
445 W. Erie
Chicago, IL 60610
312/337-8400

ABC Pictures
1867 E. Florida
Springfield, MO 65803
417/869-3456 • 417/869-9185 - fax

Bodhis Photo Service
112 W. Grand
Chicago, IL 60610
312/321-1141
312/321-3610 - fax

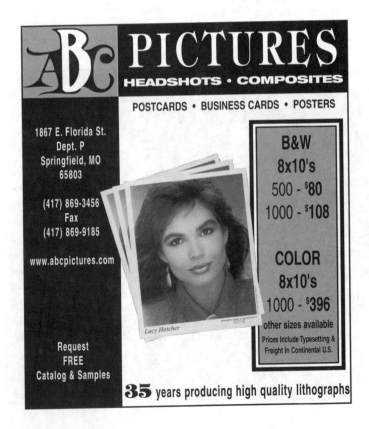

Composites International
12335 S. Keeler Avenue
Alsip, IL 60803
708/597-3449
708/597-3421 - fax

Great Graphics Photoscan
646 Bryn Mawr Street
Orlando, FL 32804
800/352-6367
407/839-5029

National Photo Service
114 W. Illinois
Chicago, IL 60610
312/644-5211
312/644-6285 - fax

Quantity Photo
Rich Pace
119 W. Hubbard 2nd floor
Chicago, IL 60610
312/644-8290
312/644-8299 - fax

Here at Quantity Photo, we've been helping actors, models, and entertainers for over 50 years. Our owner-manager, Rich Pace, alumni of Second City, brings his expertise to personally help you and oversee the production of your photos. Our hallmarks are Quality, Friendly Service, and Low Prices!

Makeup Artists

Bianco Scotti Productions
2001 W. Pershing - 5th floor
Chicago. IL 60609
312/301-9373

Cathy Durkin
1749 N. Wells #1106
Chicago, IL 60614
312/787-0848

Jeanean-Lorrece Eldridge
P.O. Box 21397
Chicago, IL 60621
773/651-5690

Robyn Goldman
1445 N. State Parkway
Chicago, IL 60610
312/751-8994

Blair Laden
1864 Sherman Avenue
Evanston, IL 60201
847/328-1177

Jerry Malik
Chicago, IL
773/525-8892

Marilyn Miglin School of Makeup
112 E. Oak Street
Chicago, IL 60611
800/662-1120 • 312/943-1184 - fax

Media Hair & Makeup Group
Maureen Kalagian
708/848-8400

Sandy Morris
773/549-4951

Suzi Ostos
Chicago, IL
773/868-1738 • 312/688-4540

Nancy P. Stanley
2426 N. Seminary
Chicago, IL 60614
773/871-1396

Perfecting your Resumé and Cover Letter

I sat me down, Devised a new commission, wrote it fair. I once did hold it, as our statists do, A baseness to write fair, and labored much How to forget that learning, but, sir, now It did me yeoman's service.

> ## Resumé:
> *n.* **1.** a brief account of one's professional or work experience and qualifications, often submitted with an employment application. **2.** a summary.

By Adrianne Duncan

A legible, clear **resumé** and a readable, effective **cover letter** are vital to your acting career. The resumé is a **one-page summary** of your acting experience. It should be divided into several main categories: theatre, film, television, commercial, industrial, education, training and special skills.

Obviously, if you have no experience in a particular area, you do not have to list that category of work on your resumé. For the categories in which you were a performer, you should list the name of the production on the left, the role you played in the middle and the theatre, studio or production company on the right. For the categories in which you received training, you can do one of two things. Either break it down into area of training (i.e. acting, voice, dance, etc.) and list your teachers correspondingly, or list the schools or studios at which you studied and note each class you took. I recommend the former for those who have more training, the latter for those who have had less opportunity to study and should highlight what they have learned.

In the **commercial** category, it is advisable to write "Commercial list available upon request" at either the bottom of your resumé or next to the commercial heading, since you can get into that sticky area of **product conflict** if you list the products you've done spots for. If you

product conflict if you list the products you've done spots for. If you have a university degree or degrees or have done college course work, you should list that under the Education heading; don't worry if you don't have a degree in theatre.

See page 126 in the Unions section for a discussion of product conflict.

The **special skills** category can include anything from the dialects you do well to the sports you play (if you play on a competitive level, indicate that; if you play recreationally, indicate that as well; if you can only stand and sit, well, just don't list anything).

An acting resumé differs from a business resumé in several important aspects. Narrative is never used on an acting resumé. Don't state career objectives or give past job descriptions. Since age is so important in this business, don't date yourself. Don't put the year in which you graduated from a program or played a role. Put your height, weight, hair and eye color and vocal range (if you are a singer) at the top of your resumé next to your name; your beeper number or a contact number should be included there as well. Some agents may ask you to remove your contact number and have their agency sticker only. I prefer to have both. The reason for this is that casting is often done after agency hours — I have been paged on a Sunday by a casting director for a Monday booking. It can happen. Also, many theatres will want to contact you directly. Most casting directors will call you through your agent anyway, but if you are called directly, be ethical about it and pass along any auditions that should come through your agent to your agent. Besides, wouldn't you rather that your agent benefit as well from your working, since work begets work?

Above all, **DO NOT LIE** on your resumé. Aside from the fact that it is one of the Ten Commandments (or something about not bearing false witness, anyway) and God will smite you, someone human could catch you. This is a small-world business in which many people know each other. There have actually been incidents in which people have falsely claimed they were in a show that was directed by the person they are now auditioning for.

You can always enhance your resumé creatively without having to resort to fabrication. If you have loads of training, highlight that. If you have a million dialects you can do, list them. Just because you don't have 50 shows under your belt doesn't mean you can't have a resumé you can be proud of.

The Actor's Tools

The one exception is if you have worked as a film extra multiple times. Choose only one or two projects to list. Being a feature film extra is not considered professional work in Chicago, and listing too many will make you look like an extra, not an actor. It's great to get a feel for what shooting a feature is like; however, don't undermine your credibility by making extra work the focus of your resumé. And don't give your extra characters names. Casting people know the difference between an extra role and a speaking role — in fact, they probably cast all the speaking roles for the film you might have been in. Audition for speaking roles in student and independent films instead; you'll gain more valuable acting experience and it will come off better on your resumé.

I cannot state strongly enough the importance of a clear, well-presented, legible resumé. I personally take the written word to heart and it pains me when I see sloppiness. The rest of the world may not be as picky as I am, but trust me — misspellings, poor grammar and awkward word flow do make a difference, consciously or subconsciously. True, the content of your resumé is more important than its appearance. However, the presentation of your resumé speaks volumes about how professionally you view yourself and take pride in your work. If you don't view yourself professionally, then how can anyone else?

The Cover Letter

The cover letter should be included in your first round of mailings to agents and casting directors. As you become more familiar with the people you are contacting, your letters can certainly become less introductory. However, let's concentrate on your initial contact letter to the agencies.

You're doing a mailing to 15 agencies. You've done your research on each one, spoken to as many people as you can to get a feel for what these agencies are like and who they represent. You've confirmed the names of the agents you'll be sending your materials to and how their names are spelled. Your headshot would make your mother weep with pride; your resumé would make me weep with pride. **Now introduce yourself.** The best way to get an agent is to have them see you acting well in a great show or have a friend who is represented by that agency recommend you.

You can also put those two things in your cover letter. Do not be afraid to name-drop in an appropriate way. "My friend Enid Muffsberry speaks highly of you" is perfectly valid. You can also give referrals. Mentioning the names of directors or teachers you've worked with who could recommend you favorably is also valid.

Look at the letter with their eyes. Remember, agents and casting directors get multiple mailings every day. Don't just say, "I want you to represent me." So does everyone else. Instead, talk about the show you're in — or the shows you've been auditioning for. Talk about the classes you're taking. Make it seem as though you have a commitment to your craft (which, hopefully, you genuinely have) and are doing something for your career every day. Don't be intimidated if you don't know who you are addressing personally. Don't lapse into self-indulgence and give your life story — keep it brief. But you should make it personal. State what your goals are and how you think this particular agency can help you achieve them. Your letter will stand out if it is sincere, neat, stylish, and gives a feel for who you are.

There is always more to learn, and there are always plenty of mistakes to make. We've all made them. But by educating yourself and using common sense, you can avoid errors and potential embarrassment. There is virtually nothing about this business that you can control. You can't control if you get an agent or not, if you get cast in that role you're dying to play or if you become a major movie star. But you can control how you present yourself. Your career is a small business, with you as the owner, manager and product. You should treat it accordingly. And with the proper tools, you should be well on your way.

Resumé Services

Act I Bookstore
2540 N. Lincoln
Chicago, IL 60614
773/348-6757
773/348-5561 - fax

Demo Tapes

Audio One, Inc.
Kirk Johnson
325 W. Huron #512
Chicago, IL 60610
312/337-5111
312/337-5125 - fax

Bobby Schiff Music Productions
363 Longcommon Road
Riverside, IL 60546
708/442-3168
708/447-3719 - fax

Bosco Productions
661 W. Lake Street
Chicago, IL 60661
312/466-9900
312/466-0201 - fax

Digitall
230 E. Ontario #302
Chicago, IL 60611
312/335-3620

Dress Rehearsals Studios, Ltd.
1840 W. Hubbard - Rear
Chicago, IL 60622
312/829-2213

Music Workshop
4900 W. 28th Place
Cicero, IL 60804
708/652-4040

Rainbow Bridge Recording
117 W. Rockland Road
Libertyville, IL 60048
847/362-4060
847/362-4653 - fax

Scanlon Swanbeck Studio
Nancy Scanlon, John Swanbeck
3354 N. Paulina #206
Chicago, IL 60657
773/281-5321

Sound Advice
Kate McClanaghan
2028 W. Potomac #2
Chicago, IL 60622
773/772-9539
773/772-9006 - fax

Sound/Video Impressions
110 S. River Road
Des Plaines, IL 60016
847/297-4360
847/297-6870 - fax

Voices On
1943 W. Belle Plaine
Chicago, IL 60613
773/528-7041

VoiceOver 101
Ray Van Steen
325 W. Huron #512
Chicago, IL 60610
312/587-1010
312/337-5125 - fax

To find a vocal or speech coach see pages 46-50.

The Actor's Tools

Reels

Absolute Video Services, Inc.
715 S. Euclid
Oak Park, IL 60302
708/386-7550 • 708/386-2322 - fax

Actor's video demo reels: We will put together a demo reel made from your clips and photos at a reasonable cost. CTA and parking convenient.

Allied Digital Technologies
1200 Thorndale Avenue
Elk Grove Village, IL 60007
847/595-2900 • 847/595-8677 - fax

Argonne Electronics
7432 N. Milwaukee
Niles, IL 60714
847/647-8877

Cinema Video Center
211 E. Grand
Chicago, IL 60611
312/644-0861
312/644-2096 - fax

ELB's Entertainment, Inc.
Eugene Barksdale
2501 N. Lincoln Avenue #198
Chicago, IL 60614-2313
800/656-1585
312/401-7178 - fax

Film to Video Labs
4330 W. Oakton
Skokie, IL 60076
847/674-4466
847/674-4463 - fax

Golan Productions
1501 N. Magnolia
Chicago, IL 60622
773/274-3456
312/642-7441 - fax

Image Lab
117 W. Rockland Road
Libertyville, IL 60048
847/362-4060
847/362-4653 - fax

Intervideo Duplication Services
3533 S. Archer
Chicago, IL 60609
773/927-9091
773/927-9211 - fax

Master Images Video Duplication
112 Carpenter Avenue
Wheeling, IL 60090
847/541-4440

Northwest Teleproductions
142 E. Ontario
Chicago, IL 60611
312/337-6000
312/337-0500 - fax

Rainbow Bridge Recording
117 W. Rockland Road
Libertyville, IL 60048
847/362-4060
847/362-4653 - fax

Renaissance Video
130 S. Jefferson
Chicago, IL 60661
312/930-5005
312/930-9030 - fax

Sound/Video Impressions
110 S. River Road
Des Plaines, IL 60016
847/297-4360
847/297-6870 - fax

Video Replay, Inc.
118 W. Grand
Chicago, IL 60610
312/467-0425
312/467-1045 - fax

Trade Papers

The following list includes publi-
cations from across the country.

Act One Reports
640 N. LaSalle #535
Chicago, IL 60610
312/787-9384

American Theatre
335 Lexington Avenue
New York, NY 10017
212/983-5230

Audition News
P.O. Box 250
Bloomingdale, IL 60108
630/894-2278
630/894-8364 - fax

Backstage
330 W. 42nd Street
New York, NY 10036
212/437-3183 - subscription line
212/536-5368 - casting line

The Actor's Tools

Backstage West
5055 Wilshire Boulevard - 6th floor
Los Angeles, CA 90036
213/525-2356

Breakdown Services, Ltd.
P.O. Box 69277
Los Angeles, CA 90069
312/276-9166

Callboard
657 Mission Street #402
San Francisco, CA 94105
415/957-1557

Casting News
P.O. Box 201
Boston, MA 02134
617/787-2991

Drama-Logue
P.O. Box 38771
Los Angeles, CA 90038
213/464-5079

Hollywood Reporter
5055 Wilshire Boulevard
Los Angeles, CA 90036
213/525-2150

The National Casting Guide
42 W. 38th Street
New York, NY 10018
212/869-2020
888/332-6700
212/354-4099 - fax

PerformInk
3223 N. Sheffield - 3rd floor
Chicago, IL 60657
773/296-4600
773/296-4621 - fax

Ross Reports Television
Television Index, Inc.
1515 Broadway
New York, NY 10036
800/817-3273

Screen Magazine
16 W. Erie
Chicago, IL 60610
312/664-5236
312/664-8425 - fax

Show Music Magazine
Goodspeed Opera House
Box 466 Goodspeed Landing
East Haddam, CT 06423-0466
860/873-8664
860/873-2329 - fax

Theatre Communications Group
355 Lexington Avenue
New York, NY 10017
212/697-5230
212/983-4847 - fax

Theatre Directories
P.O. Box 510
Dorset, VT 05251
802/867-2223
802/867-0144 - fax

Variety
P.O. Box 6400
Torrence, CA 90504
800/323-4345
800/552-3632

Answering Services

Hate Ameritech? Here are some other options.

Burke Communications
P.O. Box 4152
Oak Park, IL 60303-4152
708/383-8580
708/386-1336 - fax

Chicagoland Answering Service
4318 N. Oak Park Avenue
Harwood Heights, IL 60634
708/867-0570

Cell Phones

Ameritech
Various Locations
Chicago, IL
800/MOBILE-1

Metrotone Paging
3321 N. Milwaukee
Chicago, IL 60641
733/777-4555

AT&T
888/344-3332

Nextel
800/NEXTEL9

Cellular One
800/CELLONE

Nova Cellular
800/571-6682

Custom Pagers of Chicago
1816 W. Irving Park
Chicago, IL 60613
773/296-4CPC

Prime Co.
900 N. Michigan Avenue - 6th floor
Chicago, IL 60611
312/943-3290

Comm One Wireless
1437 W. Taylor
Chicago, IL 60607
312/850-9400

The Sound Advantage
2911 N. Clark
Chicago, IL 60657
773/404-1288

Skynet
773/296-2200 • 312/587-3200

Makeup Supplies

A Magical Mystery Tour
6010 W. Dempster
Morton Grove, IL 60053
847/966-5090
847/966-7280 - fax

All Dressed Up Costumes
150 S. Water
Batavia, IL 60510
630/879-5130
630/879-3374 - fax

Broadway Costumes, Inc.
954 W. Washington - 4th floor
Chicago, IL 60607
312/829-6400
312/829-8621 - fax

Center Stage
497 Route 59, Aurora, IL 60504
630/851-9191

Chicago Hair Goods Co., Inc.
2405 N. Milwaukee
Chicago, IL 60647
773/384-1474

Focusing primarily on wigs.

Drum Gift Shoppe
5216 N. Clark
Chicago, IL 60640
773/769-5551

Fantasy Headquarters
4065 N. Milwaukee
Chicago, IL 60641
773/777-0222

Grand Stage Lighting Company
630 W. Lake
Chicago, IL 60661
312/332-5611

Josie O'Kain Costume & Theatre Shop
2419 B West Jefferson Street
Joliet, IL 60435
815/741-9303
815/741-9316 - fax

Razzle Dazzle Costumes
1038 Lake Street
Oak Park, IL 60301
708/383-5962
708/383-0069 - fax

Riley's Trick & Novelty Shop
6442 W. 111th
Worth, IL 60482
708/448-0075
708/448-0999 - fax

Sheet Music

Act I Bookstore
2540 N. Lincoln
Chicago, IL 60614
773/348-6757
773/348-5561 - fax

Carl Fisher Music
312 S. Wabash
Chicago, IL 60604
312/427-6652

Lighting Equipment

Chicago Spotlight, Inc.
1658 W. Carroll Avenue
Chicago, IL 60612
312/455-1171

Design Lab
806 N. Peoria - 2nd floor
Chicago, IL 60622

312/738-3305
312/738-2402 - fax

Grand Stage
630 W. Lake Street
Chicago, IL 60661
312/332-5611
312/258-0056 - fax

Dance Supplies

American Dance Center Ballet Co.
10464 W. 163rd Place
Orland Park, IL 60462
708/747-4969
708/747-0424 - fax

Big N Little Shoes
3142 W. 111th
Chicago, IL 60655
773/239-6066

Dance & Mime Shop
643 W. Grand Avenue
Chicago, IL 60610
312/666-4406

Illinois Theatrical
P.O. Box 34284
Chicago, IL 60634
773/745-7777

Kling's Theatrical Shoe Company
218 S. Wabash - 8th floor
Chicago, IL 60604
312/427-2028
312/427-3929 - fax

Motion Unlimited
218 S. Wabash - 8th floor
Chicago, IL 60604
312/922-3330

Show Off
1472 Elmhurst Road
Elk Grove Village, IL 60007
847/439-0206
847/439-0219 - fax

Costume Shops

A Lost Eras Costumes & Props
Charlotte Walters
1511 W. Howard
Chicago, IL 60626
773/764-7400
773/764-7433 - fax

A Magical Mystery Tour
6010 W. Dempster
Morton Grove, IL 60053
847/966-5090
847/966-7280 - fax

All Dressed Up Costumes
150 S. Water
Batavia, IL 60510
630/879-5130
630/879-3374 - fax

Bead Different
214 E. Chicago Avenue
Westmont, IL 60559
630/323-1962

Beatnix
3400 N. Halsted
Chicago, IL 60657
773/281-6933

Beverly Costume Shop
11628 S. Western
Chicago, IL 60643
773/779-0068
773/779-2434 - fax

The Actor's Tools

Broadway Costumes, Inc.
954 W. Washington - 4th floor
Chicago, IL 60607
312/829-6400
312/829-8621 - fax

Center Stage
497 Route 59
Aurora, IL 60504
630/851-9191

Chicago Costume Company
1120 W. Fullerton
Chicago, IL 60614
773/528-1264
773/935-4197 - fax

Cindy Makes Things
627 S. Western
Park Ridge, IL 60068
847/696-1685

Dance & Mime Shop
643 W. Grand Avenue
Chicago, IL 60610
312/666-4406

Drum Gift Shoppe
5216 N. Clark
Chicago, IL 60640
773/769-5551

Facemakers, Inc.
140 Fifth Street
Savannah, IL 61074
815/273-3944

Fantasy Headquarters
4065 N. Milwaukee
Chicago, IL 60641
773/777-0222

Flashy Trash
3524 N. Halsted
Chicago, IL 60657
773/327-6900
773/327-9736 - fax

Josie O'Kain Costume & Theatre Shop
2419 B West Jefferson Street
Joliet, IL 60435
815/741-9303
815/741-9316 - fax

Ken Young Antiques
920 Green Bay Road
Winnetka, IL 60093
847/441-6670

Leo's Dancewear
1900 N. Narragansett
Chicago, IL 60639
773/745-5600

Razzle Dazzle Costumes
1038 Lake Street
Oak Park, IL 60301
708/383-5962
708/383-0069 - fax

Task Force Military
2341 W. Belmont
Chicago, IL 60618
773/477-7096

Victorian Emphasis
918 Green Bay Road
Winnetka, IL 60093
847/441-6675

Wild Thing
2933 N. Clark
Chicago, IL 60657
773/549-7787

Thrift Stores

Ark Thrift Shop
3345 N. Lincoln
Chicago, IL 60657
773/248-1117

Bargains Unlimited
3119 N. Lincoln Avenue
Chicago, IL 60657
773/525-8595

Chicago Recycle Shop
5308 N. Clark
Chicago, IL 60640
773/878-8525

County Faire Antiques
Furniture & Furnishings/Stage Sets
961 N. Milwaukee (at Inverrary)
Wheeling, IL 60090
847/537-9987

Dandelion
2117 N. Damen
Chicago, IL 60647
773/862-9333

Disgraceland
3330 N. Clark
Chicago, IL 60657
773/281-5875

Flashback Collectables
3450 N. Clark
Chicago, IL 60657
773/929-5060

Goodwill Industries
3039 N. Pulaski
Chicago, IL 60641
773/286-4744

Howard Brown Memorial
Clinic Resale Shop
3651 N. Halsted
Chicago, IL 60657
773/549-5943

Hubba Hubba
3338 N. Clark
Chicago, IL 60657
773/477-1414

Kismet Vintage Clothing and Furniture
2923 N. Southport
Chicago, IL 60657
773/528-4497

Little City Resale Shop
1720 W. Algonquin
Palatine, IL 60067
847/358-5510
847/358-3291 - fax

Make Us An Offer
6459 S. Cottage Grove
Chicago, IL 60637
773/667-1295
773/667-8643 - fax

Ragstock
812 W. Belmont - 2nd floor
Chicago, IL 60657
773/868-9263
773/868-6819 - fax

Right Place
5219 N. Clark
Chicago, IL 60640
773/561-7757

Salvation Army Thrift Store
3837 W. Fullerton
Chicago, IL 60647
773/276-1955

Threads
1400 N. Milwaukee
Chicago, IL 60622
773/276-6411

Time Well Spent Thrift Shop
2780 N. Lincoln
Chicago, IL 60614
773/549-2113

Unique Thrift Store
3224 S. Halsted
Chicago, IL 60608
312/842-8123

White Elephant Shop
Children's Memorial Hospital
2380 N. Lincoln Avenue
Chicago, IL 60614
773/281-3747

> Check out the Living section for lists of goods and services that all actors need.

Libraries

Harold Washington Public Library
400 S. State Street
Chicago, IL 60610
312/747-4300

Newberry Library
60 W. Walton Street
Chicago, IL 60610
312/943-9090

North Suburban Library System
847/459-1300

Rand McNally Library
8255 N. Central Park Avenue
Skokie, IL 60076
847/673-9100

Stock Montage
921 W. Van Buren #201
Chicago, IL 60607
312/733-3239

Sulzer Regional Library
4455 N. Lincoln
Chicago, IL 60625
312/744-7616

Women's Bureau
U.S. Department of Labor
230 S. Dearborn
Chicago, IL 60604
312/353-6985
312/353-6986 - fax

Bookstores

Act I Bookstore
2540 N. Lincoln
Chicago, IL 60614
773/348-6757
773/348-5561 - fax

Aspidistra Bookshop
2630 N. Clark
Chicago, IL 60614
773/549-3129

Barbara's Bookstore
1350 N. Wells
Chicago, IL 60610
312/642-5044

Barnes and Noble Bookstore
659 W. Diversey
Chicago, IL 60614
773/871-9004
773/871-5893 - fax

Unabridged Books
3251 N. Broadway
Chicago, IL 60657
773/883-9119
773/883-9559 - fax

Casting Hotlines

The latest auditions are put on these hotlines first. The Audition Hotline and Casting Call Hotline are updated twice weekly.

Audition Hotline
312/409-9900

Casting Call Hotline
P.O. Box 59232
Hoffman Estates, IL 60159
976-CAST
847/885-4522
847/885-7810 - fax

Illinois Filmboard Hotline
Chicago, IL
312/427-FILM

Call 976-CAST for the latest audition notices. 30 cents a minute. Anywhere in Chicago. The Casting Call Hotline

Actor's Equity Association also has a hotline for its members. Check out page 117 for information on Actor's Equity.

The Actor's Tools

Talent and Casting Agencies

What do agents do? How do they work? How can I get signed? Once I'm signed, how can I get them to send me out? Then there are casting directors. What's up with them? What's the difference between a casting director and a talent agent? For that matter, what if I'm a writer and I'm looking for someone to represent my work? What agencies in the city do that?

The answers to many of these questions and others lie within. Read on, grasshopper.

The Secrets of
getting an Agent

Why may not that be the skull of an agent? Where be his quiddities now, his quillities, his files, his tenures and his tricks?

Agent:
n. **1.** a person or firm authorized to act. **2.** a spy. **3.** a substance that causes a reaction. **4.** a means or instrument.

By Adrianne Duncan

Agents. If you want to be a working, successful actor in Chicago, you must have one. Period. Many of you reading this probably have an agent or two, but feel like you don't — as though you've been swallowed up by the filing cabinets at Emilia Lorence, never to be seen again. How many of you have dropped by or called to check in with your agent, only to be met with a blank stare or "Your name is..." That's not a great actor-agent relationship. You should have a rapport with these people beyond just being registered with them.

Your **relationship** with your agent or agents can only be enhanced by having a firm understanding of what they do. Agents can be intimidating. You feel like you're bugging them, like they don't know who you are, like they do nothing for you. Or you can't get one at all. Hopefully this discussion will give you a better idea of how you can get an agent, and how you can enhance your relationship with the agents you already have.

An agent is the middleman between you the casting director, who is then the middleman between the agent and the client. That client could be an ad agency, a theatre, a studio, a network or a production company. An agent takes a commission from you of 10 percent of your gross profit from the jobs they directly get for you. In print work, the commission is 20 percent. Any agency that attempts to gather a commission of more than 10 percent (or 20 percent for print) is not legitimate and should be reported to the unions or the Illinois Department of Labor.

See page 129 for a discussion of what to do to protect yourself.

An agent does *not* try to get you to have your pictures taken for an exorbitant fee with a certain photographer or take a particular class — that is a scam as well. An agent cannot guarantee you work, nor can they create jobs for you. Their function is to recommend you to people in a position to cast you. Most often, that recommendation comes in the form of submitting your headshot and resumé based on the specifics of a role or project. Ideally, an agent is also someone who can manage and guide your career, who has foresight about what you should be doing in the long run rather than just trying to get you paying jobs regardless of what those jobs are.

The Pecking Order

It behooves you to understand as much as you can about what your agent does, and also what other industry professionals do and how your job as an actor is related to theirs. Let's look at the pecking order by going through a casting call for a commercial.

A **Client** (a company that has goods or services to sell) hires an **Ad Agency** to make an advertisement for its **Product.** The Ad Agency hires a **Production Company** to physically make the commercial. They then hire a **Casting Director** (they may have one in-house) who then calls the **Agent** with the **Specs** (type, age, gender, etc.) for each role. The Casting Director may also request to see certain specific **actors**. The Agent then calls the Actor.

The audition process will normally consist of an **Audition,** in which you will be videotaped reading **Copy** (the script or portions of it from the commercial). For the **Callback,** you will most likely do the same thing, but the **Client** will probably be present.

For a film or television audition, the sequence of events is similar. Here, the **Studio** hires a **Director** for its project. A Casting Director is then hired, who calls the Agent, and from then on the process is pretty much the same.

So, as you can see, the client is on top, the casting director and agent are in the lower middle, and the actor is pretty much on the bottom of

Agencies

the totem pole. That's why you need an agent, and why you should understand his or her job.

Getting an Agent

For those bemoaning the fact that you don't yet have an agent, realize one hard truth. **In Chicago, it is easy to get an agent** compared to New York or Los Angeles. It's cake. In those cities, it is next to impossible. Here, many agencies will represent you with an interview only, and some by only seeing your picture. In New York, that is unheard of. For many agents there, auditioning for them in their office with a monologue or a scene is not enough — they want to see you in a show. Then, once you're cast in a show, they're too busy to come.

On the coasts, you must sign with one agent only. You can free-lance with multiple agents for a short period of time, but any reputable agent will want you to sign with them if you're working well together after a few months. Additionally, both cities make a distinction between commercial work (anything in which you would actually sell a product), for which you need a commercial agent, and theatre, film and television, for which you need a theatrical agent. You can only have one of each.

In Chicago, we have a different system called **multi-listing.** Here, actors have the choice of being represented by one or multiple agents. There are advantages and disadvantages to both, which we'll discuss shortly.

Tools and Strategies

It's **mailing time,** boys and girls! There are some basic things that should be in every mailing: good quality headshots; a readable, attractive resumé that shows you off to your best advantage (regardless of the amount of work you may have actually done); and a cover letter with something to say.

See *The Actor's Tools,* starting on page 55, for more advice on these subjects.

Find out as much as possible about each agency before doing your mailing. If you're Caucasian, realize that Salazar & Navas and ETA represent mostly minority performers. Find out the differences between agencies: Geddes is a smaller, managerial-style agency with an office in Los Angeles; Emilia Lorence is one of Chicago's oldest and largest agencies with bigger departments but less personal attention. Find out which agencies are non-union (McBlaine & Associates, Talent Group) and which are union franchised (most of the other ones). Find out the proper spelling of the agents' names you are writing and whether they are, in fact, still with the agency — agents can be somewhat transient and staying informed can only help you. Check out the agent listings in this section and pick up an Act One Reports to supplement this book, as agents change jobs throughout the year. Again, knowing as much as possible about what agents do is empowering and helps level the playing field. It also keeps you from making a faux pas that could make an agent remember you in an unflattering way.

You've done your mailing, and three agencies have expressed an interest in you. One wants 30 pictures and resumés and is ready to work with you. One wants to sit down and talk with you. And a third wants you to come in for an interview and an audition. The first is easy enough — the last is a little harder.

For the **audition**, prepare at least two or three monologues, even if they only ask for one. Ask them what their preference is — they'll almost certainly want to see contemporary pieces. Since Chicago agencies work primarily with on-camera projects as opposed to theatre, try to find pieces as filmic as possible, ones that will show who you are to the agent. Play close to home; the agent wants to see who they're getting. If they've asked you to read commercial copy, prepare at home. Watch commercials. Pay attention to actors' delivery. Practice with newspaper or magazine ad copy, and realize that they will probably tape you, so practice as though you are on-camera.

As far as the interview goes, try to remember that you are just as an important a link in the chain as they are. It's almost impossible, but don't *need* anything from them. Figure out who you are and what you can bring to the table. Watch television, plays, commercials, movies. It may not always seem the case, but you are in fact the agent's client — not the other way around. *You* pay *them*. It is my staunch belief that agents and actors are equals in this business. Ideally, we are colleagues. Try to see things from their perspective and the business through their eyes. And bring that to the interview.

Building a Relationship

When you do register with an agent or agents, be aware of the **nature of your relationship**. If your relationship is new or distant and you're trying to get noticed, be appropriate. Don't ingratiate yourself with them. Be sensitive. Make sure you know your agency's policy on drop-ping by and checking in. If you're calling to check in, make sure you have a legitimate reason for doing so. Something as simple as "Hi, this is Bob Actor and I'm calling to see if you have enough of my pictures and resumés" is vastly preferable to "Hey, what's up?" Remember, agents are busy people and we want them to be. When they work, we work. But don't be afraid of them either. If you are called for an audi-tion, you have every right to get all the information you need — if there is copy or not, location, dress, shoot date, etc. — before you let your agent off the phone. Let them know if you haven't met certain casting directors. Inform them when you're going out of town — this is known as "booking out." Don't feel silly doing it even if you haven't been called in three months; if you don't, chances are that's the week you'll be called. And besides, it gives you an excuse to check in.

Also, educate yourself as much as possible about **protocol**. Getting your agent mad at you is not a good thing. For example, you must be aware of your union status. Do not audition for a union job if you are a must-join and cannot afford the initiation fee. Currently, joining fees for AFTRA and Equity are $800, while SAG's joining fee is $1,080. Well worth it in the long run, but you must produce these fees up front *before* you can perform the job for which you have been hired. If you are booked and can't join, this will be a horrendous situation for all involved. Be honest and up front with your agent; if you can't or don't want to join the unions, let them know.

See page 116 for a discussion of unions.

To Be (Exclusive) or Not To Be

So you've had your three agents for a while now, and you're wondering if you should go exclusive with one of them. What are the advantages and disadvantages of being **multi-listed versus being exclusive** in Chicago? If you're multi-listed, you maximize your potential to expose yourself to the largest number of job opportunities. Not all agents are called for all projects; some ad agencies and casting directors work with only a few agencies. If you are a new performer, you will expose yourself to more people in the industry by being multi-listed, especially before your name becomes familiar to the casting directors. Also, by multi-listing, you can find the agent who fits you best, and the agency where you feel the most at home.

Being exclusive has its advantages as well. It's a bit more prestigious; having somebody want to stake his or her claim on you does make you more attractive to those in a position to cast you. You have more of an opportunity to be managed and given personal attention. You're more likely to be consistently submitted, since you'll be more at the forefront of your agent's mind than multi-listed actors. An agent has more of a responsibility to an exclusive talent than to a multi-listed one. That additional responsibility rests on the actor's shoulders as well.

In short, being exclusive versus being multi-listed is a highly personal decision and often simply a matter of preference. It's like dating before you get married. Dating is great — it's fun, you meet lots of cool people, you get to go out a lot, and then you get your heart stomped on and wind up bitter and confused (oops, too much information). Seriously, it *is* like dating in that you get to scope out the feel of each agency and what they have to offer. It is possible to form good relationships at several agencies and work profitably on that basis.

However, if you do have good relationships with your agents, chances are that at least one of them will ask you to go exclusive at some point. This is a matter that should be handled as professionally as possible, but it should be understood that feelings will be involved on both sides. If you want to go exclusive, great! Sign on the dotted line, go and tell your other agents and collect your pictures — and be aware that the decision will likely be more complex than that. If you don't want to go exclusive with this particular agency, be sensitive to how they may react. How would you feel if you asked someone to marry you and they said no? Be aware of the fact that your relationship may change. It is absolutely your right to handle your career as you see fit; however, the agent may feel that they are devoting so much time and energy to you that they deserve to be in a reciprocal relationship.

You really can't work without an agent. And you shouldn't have to — you have enough to worry about without constantly having to scrounge up jobs for yourself. There are a lot of terrific, talented people in Chicago that choose to work as agents. Hopefully, you'll get a chance to work with them. This business is fascinating; learning as much as you can about it will benefit you immensely as an actor, and it happens to be interesting as well. Good luck!

Talent Agencies

Ambassador Talent
333 N. Michigan #1000
Chicago, IL 60601
312/641-3491
SAG/AFTRA/AFM franchised
Attn. Susan: agent/associate

Registration Policy: Send headshot and resumé. All ages.

Audition Policy: Will call if interested.

Aria Model and Talent Management
1017 W. Washington #2C
Chicago, IL 60607
312/243-9400
312/243-9020 - fax
SAG/AFTRA/Equity franchised

Mary Boncher: co-owner

Marie Anderson Boyd: co-owner

Carrie Johnson: on-camera, TV, film

Christina Hansen: TV, Film

Melanie Bhasin: print

Kelly Cleveland: men's fashion director

Chadwick Godfrey: hair & makeup

David Love: women's fashion director

Sebastian McWilliams: creative director

Anna Reigh: runway director

Registration Policy: Actors/models must submit resumé and photo/composite by mail. Agency will contact you, if interested.

Audition Policy: Agency will call if interested. DO NOT CALL.

Check In Policy: Varies

Affiliates: NY/ LA

Arlene Wilson Models
430 W. Erie #210
Chicago, IL 60610
312/573-0200
312/573-0046 - fax
AFTRA/SAG/Equity franchised

Michael Stothard: President

Peter Forster: on-camera

Anna Jordan: on-camera, voice-over

Laura Alexander: children, on-camera, commercial print

Bill Allen: office manager

Shane Allen: new face director

Dan Deely: agency director

Lisa Goren: children

Registration Policy: Submit headshot and resumé by mail first. The agency will contact you, if interested.

Audition Policy: Agency will call if interested.

Affiliates: Milwaukee and Atlanta

Baker & Rowley
Heartbreak Lofts
17 N. Loomis #1B
Chicago, IL 60607
773/252-7900
773/252-8014 - fax
AFTRA/SAG franchised

Diane Rowley: director

Richard Baker: agent

Roberta Kablach: agent

A. Ashley Hoff: talent scout

on-camera, film, print, voice-over, tradeshow, promotions

Registration Policy: Send 5 headshots and resumés and voice demo with a SASE. Agent will contact you if interested. Multicultural representation. Open registration Tuesdays, 12-2pm. No other drop-ins.

Audition Policy: Will call if interested.

CED (Cunningham, Escott, DiPene)
1 E. Superior Street #505
Chicago, IL 60611
312/944-5600
312/944-9746 - VO
312/944-5694 - fax
SAG/AFTRA/Equity franchised

Diane Herro Sanford: on-camera, stage

Gina Mazza: voice-over

Tina O'Brien: children

Monica Valdean: industrial & children

Registration Policy: Send photo/resumé, demo. Agent will call if interested. Representing only exclusive clients.

Affiliates: NY/LA

Chicago Live Models, Inc.
Box 6044
Buffalo Grove, IL 60089
847/540-7400
847/540-7423 - fax

Sherri Hicks: President

Actors, dancers, models, pagent title holders - no children under 3

Registration Policy: H/R and composites, resumé, demo tapes

Audition Policy: Agency will call if interested.

Check In Policy: Check for details.

Joy Dickens
9236 N. Springfield
Evanston, IL 60203
847/677-2643
847/667-2654 - fax

Elite Model Management
58 W. Huron
Chicago, IL 60610
312/943-3226
312/943-2590 - fax

Emilia Lorence Agency
325 W. Huron Street #404
Chicago, IL 60610
312/787-2033
312/787-5239 - fax
AFTRA/SAG/Equity franchised
Emilia Lorence: on-camera, industrial, film
Nick DeBok: on-camera, print
Jackie Grimes: on-camera, voice-over
Judy Kasner: on-camera, industrial, feature film, TV
Vicki Choconas: convention, trade-show
Registration Policy: Open registration on Mon., Wed., Fri., 10:00-11:30am and 2:30pm-4pm. Closed daily between 12:00 & 2:00. Actors should bring 3 headshots and resumés. Voice-over talent should submit a tape.
Audition Policy: Will call if interested.
Check In Policy: Anyday
Affiliates: NY/LA

ETA, Inc.
7558 S. Chicago Avenue
Chicago, IL 60619
773/752-3955 • 773/752-8727 - fax
SAG/AFTRA franchised
Joan P. Brown: President
Registration Policy: Send H/R.
Audition Policy: Will call if interested.

Geddes Agency
1633 N. Halsted #400
Chicago, IL 60614
312/787-8333
312/787-6677 - fax
AFTRA/SAG/Equity franchised
Elizabeth Geddes: film, TV, theatre
Paula Muzik: film, TV, theatre
Polly Rich: commercial, industrial
Beth-Ann Zeitler: voice-over
Registration Policy: Actors must submit headshot and resumé by mail only. Agency will call if interested.
Check In Policy: None
Affiliates: LA

Harrise Davidson & Associates
65 E. Wacker Place #2401
Chicago, IL 60601
312/782-4480
312/782-3363 - fax
AFTRA/SAG/Equity franchised
Harrise Davidson: President
Stacey Shafer: commercial, film, TV
Gina Wake: industrial, film, promotions
Jen Barnett: children
Jennifer Bowland: voice-over
Mauri Paige: print, promotions
Registration Policy: Open registration on Wednesday from 3-4pm. Can also submit H/R, composite by mail. No walk ins.
Audition Policy: Will call if interested.
Check In Policy: Phone. Prefer through mail.

Jefferson and Associates
1050 N. State Street
Chicago, IL 60610
312/337-1930
312/337-7398 - fax
AFTRA/SAG/Equity franchised
Pamela Jefferson: voice-over
Chuck Saucier: on-camera, commercial, TV, film
Registration Policy: Represents exclusive talent only. Actors must submit headshot and resumé by mail.
Audition Policy: Will contact you to make an appointment if interested.

Karen Stavins Enterprises, Inc.
Three Illinois Center
303 E. Wacker - Concourse
Chicago, IL 60601
312/938-1140
Registration Policy: Submit picture and resumé, composites or voice tapes. Attn: New Talent. Non-union talent booked for commercials, industrials, TV/film, voice-over, trade shows, live shows. 17 years and older. Respond within 6 months.
Audition policy: Agency will call if interested.
Check in policy: None.

Lily's Talent Agency, Inc.
5962 N. Elston
Chicago, IL 60646
773/792-1160
773/792-0939 - fax
AFTRA/SAG/Equity franchised

Lily Ho: President

Angela Jackson: print

Theresa Cunningham: promotions

Registration Policy: Actors must submit two headshots and resumés and SASE by mail. Include phone number and statistics.

Audition Policy: Agency will respond if interested.

Check In Policy: Check in every 3-4 months to make sure you have enough headshots on file.

Linda Jack Talent
230 E. Ohio #200
Chicago, IL 60611
312/587-1155
312/587-2122 - fax
AFTRA/ SAG franchised

Linda Jack: voice-over

Linda Bernasconi: on-camera

Erica Daniels: on-camera

Mickey Grossman: on-camera

Jamie Marchi: voice-over

Stephanie Newman: voice-over

Registration Policy: Submission by mail. No walk-ins.

Audition Policy: Will call if interested.

Check In Policy: By phone once a week.

Matson-McCall
7221 Oak Avenue
Gary, IN 46403
219/938-1280

Registration Policy: Send H/R.

Audition Policy: Will call if interested.

McBlaine & Associates, Inc.
515 N. Northwest Highway
Park Ridge, IL 60068
847/823-3877
847/823-1253 - fax

Paige Ehlman: talent agent

Registration Policy: No drop-ins. Send a headshot and resumé with a SASE.

Audition policy: Agency will call if interested.

Check in policy: Wednesday afternoons once a month.

McCall Model & Talent
6933 S. Crandon #4C
Chicago, IL 60649
773/667-0611
773/667-0636 - fax

Rochelle McCall: voice-over, commercial, print, industrials

Registration Policy: Extras - Appt. only. Send headshot or color snapshot (preferred) and resumé to: Attn: Extras Casting. Include age, height, hair and eye color.

Check in policy: Once a month.

Affiliates: LA

Mira Modeling & Promotion, Inc.
P.O. Box 95704
Hoffman Estates, IL 60195
800/982-MIRA
847/519-1159 - fax

Christian Conti: President/CEO

Sarkis Danavi: VP of Operations

Registration Policy: Models send H/R or composite to agency. Will respond if interested.

Audition Policy: Will call if interested.

Affiliates: West Palm Beach

Agencies

Nicosia Entertainment Enterprises

305 W. Hackberry Drive
Arlington Heights, IL 60004
847/392-9259

Registration policy: H/R, demo tapes, video. Send SASE. No phone calls.

Audition policy: Will call if interested.

Norman Schucart Enterprises

1417 Green Bay Road
Highland Park, IL 60035
847/433-1113
847/433-1113 - fax
AFTRA/SAG franchised

Norman Schucart: TV, industrial, film, print, live shows

Nancy Elliott: TV, industrial, film, print, live shows

Registration Policy: New talent should first submit headshot/composite and resumé with phone number by mail (include SASE postcard). If interested, the agency will arrange to interview you in Chicago.

Audition Policy: Agency will call if interested.

North Shore Talent, Inc.

454 Peterson Road
Libertyville, IL 60048
847/816-1811 • 847/816-1717 - fax

Kerstin Schaefer: on-camera, voice-over, print, promotion, convention

Sherrill Tripp: on-camera, voice-over, print, promotion, convention

Registration Policy: Talent check-in line 847/816-1819. Submit headshot, resumé and any marketing materials (non-returnable). Registration by appt. only. No drop-ins.

Check In Policy: Registered talent only call 847/816-1819 Thursday between 12-3pm.

Audition Policy: Agency will call if interested.

Sa-Rah Talent
222 S. Morgan #2C
Chicago, IL 60607
312/733-2822
312/733-1529 - fax
AFTRA/SAG franchised

Jacquelyn Conard: voice-over, print, commercial, film, industrial

Registration Policy: Mail 3-5 photos and resumés with SASE. No drop-ins.

Check In Policy: Call once a week.

Audition Policy: Will call if interested.

Salazar & Navas, Inc.
760 N. Ogden #2200
Chicago, IL 60622
312/666-1677
312/666-1681 - fax
AFTRA/SAG franchised

Myrna Salazar: on-camera, voice-over, film, commercial, print

Trina Navas: on-camera, voice-over, film, commercial, print

Susan Acuna: on-camera, voice-over, film, commercial, print

Registration Policy: Hispanic/Latin types preferred, but all types considered and represented. New talent seen on Tuesday, 10-4pm. Call if interested.

Check In Policy: Once a week.

Shirley Hamilton, Inc.
333 E. Ontario #302B
Chicago, IL 60611
312/787-4700
312/787-8456 - fax
AFTRA/SAG/Equity franchised

Shirley Hamilton: President

Lynn Hamilton: Vice President

Tracey Park: TV, film, voice-over

Mari Mask: TV, film, voice-over

Darrell Copeland: print, trade show

Registration Policy: Registration by mail only with SASE. Actors must submit headshot and resumé. Agency will contact by mail if interested.

Check In Policy: Phone or in person except between 12:30- 2:30pm.

Stewart Talent
58 W. Huron
Chicago, IL 60610
312/943-0892 - adults
312/943-3131 - kids
312/943-2590 - fax
AFTRA/SAG/Equity franchised

Jane Stewart: President

Maureen Brookman: TV, stage, film

Maryann Drake: TV, stage, film

Nancy Kidder: industrial, film

Joan Sparks: voice-over

Wade Childress: commercial, print

Kathi Gardner: children, print

Elizabeth Oldroyd: children

Sheila Dougherty: children, commercials

Registration Policy: Submit H/R. Agency will contact within 6-8 weeks if interested.

Audition Policy: Will call within 6-8 weeks if interested.

Suzanne's A-Plus
108 W. Oak
Chicago, IL 60610
312/642-8151
312/803-1368 - info line
312/943-9751 - fax
AFTRA/SAG/WGA franchised

Suzanne Johnson: owner

Robert Schroeder: on-camera

Tracy Kaplan: on-camera

Marsha Becker: children, print, on-camera

Katherine Tenerowicz: print

Amy Leften: print

Claudine Klutter: runway

Registration Policy: Actors must submit photo and resumé, Attn: "on-camera." Models call Thursday to come in on Friday. Open call for models M-F 10-12pm, 1-4pm. Also call info line.

Audition Policy: Will contact within 6-8 weeks if interested.

Agencies

Talent Group
4637 N. Magnolia
Chicago, IL 60640
773/561-8814 • 773/728-5896 - fax
Registration Policy: No drop-ins. Send a headshot and resumé or voice-over tape addressed to Annette Dariano.
Check In Policy: Once a month.
Audition Policy: Agency will call if interested.

Third Coast Artist
641 W. Lake Street #402
Chicago, IL 60661
312/707-8700 • 312/707-8515 - fax
AFTRA/SAG/Equity franchised
Pam Whitfield: President
Registration Policy: Actors, please submit pictures and resumés to the Commercial Department. Open call Tues. 9:30-10:00a.m. for fashion models only (height req. women 5'9"-5'11," men 5'11"-6'1").
Check in policy: Once a week by phone.
Audtion policy: Agency will call if interested.

TRC Productions
910 Skokie Highway #106
Northbrook, IL 60062
847/480-1666
847/480-7336 - fax
Registration Policy: Phone or submit H/R by mail.

Voices Unlimited
541 N. Fairbanks Court #2850
Chicago, IL 60611
312/832-1113
AFTRA/SAG franchised
Sharon Wottrich: President
Linda Bracilano: voice-over
Susan Davies: voice-over
Registration Policy: Voice-over talent should submit commercial and/or narrative tape, 2 min. or less with resumé.
Audition Policy: Agency will call if interested.

Talent Agents - Milwaukee

Arlene Wilson Talent, Inc.
807 N. Jefferson #200
Milwaukee, WI 53202
414/283-5600
414/283-5610 - fax
AFTRA franchised
Michael Stothard: President
Catherine Hagen: agency director
Carol Rathe: voice-over, on-camera, broadcast director
Coni Flowler: print, new talent, children's director.
Registration Policy: Wednesday 1:30-3 open call for actors with headshot/resumé or voice talent with tape. Send H/R ONLY IF you cannot come to the open call.
Audition Policy: Open call on Wednesday.
Check In Policy: Every 2 weeks Tuesday-Thursday.

Jennifer's Talent Unlimited, Inc.
740 N. Plankinton #300
Milwaukee, WI 53203
414/277-9440
414/277-0918 - fax
AFTRA franchised
Jennifer L. Berg: president
Jan Brethauer, Marna Reardon: broadcast
Stacy Hanert: print
Registration Policy: Actors must submit a headshot and resumé.
Audition Policy: Agency will call if interested.
Check In Policy: Check in every week.
Affiliates: LA

Lori Lins, Ltd.
7611 W. Holmes
Green Field, WI 53220
414/282-3500
414/282-3404 - fax
AFTRA/SAG franchised
Lori Lins: booker

Monnie Schrader: booker
Betty Anthoine: booker
Registration Policy: Actors must submit headshot and resumé.
Audition Policy: Agency will call if interested.
Check In Policy: Monthly

Tradeshow Agencies

A-Z Entertainment Ltd.
600 Northgate Parkway #L
Wheeling, IL 60090
847/537-5100
847/537-6390 - fax
Registration Policy: Submit H/R to Kori. Especially seeking emcees, dancers, and specialty performers.
Audition Policy: Agency will call for audition/interview if interested.

All About Models Talent & Promotions, Inc.
222 W. Huron #4003
Chicago, IL 60610
312/573-0500
312/573-0566 - fax
Registration Policy: Open registration on Thursday 1-5 pm or submit H/R by mail.
Check In Policy: Once a week.
Audition Policy: Come to open registration

or agency will call you if submitted by mail.
Affiliates: NY/LA

Best Faces
1152 N. Lasalle #F
Chicago, IL 60610
312/944-3009
312/944-7006 - fax
Registration Policy: Send materials Attn: Judy Mudd
Audition Policy: Will contact if interested.
Check In Policy: Every 2/3 weeks

Chicago Images
925 N. Milwaukee Avenue #137
Wheeling, IL 60090
847/465-8881
847/465-8884 - fax
Registration Policy: Submit H/R. Agency will call if interested. DO NOT CALL THEM.

Agencies

Claire Model & Talent Management
P.O. Box 1028
Wheeling, IL 60090
847/459-4242
Registration Policy: Send H/R to Clarisse Rosenstock.

Check In Policy: Monthly

Audition Policy: Will call in for look-see/ audition if type is needed.

Affiliates: Affinity (LA), Claire Model & Talent (NY)

Claire Model & Talent Management has been serving clients throughout Chicagoland and across the nation since 1989. We represent attractive, outgoing adult talent for trade shows, promotions, print, fashion, film, and TV. We are registering models who are attractive and outgoing. Professional attitude and dependability are a must!

Excel Model & Talent Management
Box 1425
LaGrange Park , IL 60526
708/442-9227
Registration Policy: Submit H/R. Agency will call if interested. NO CALLS.

Group, Ltd.
2375 E. Tropicana #E
Las Vegas, NV 89119
702/895-8926
Registration Policy: Submit H/R to Vegas office. Will contact if interested.

Affiliates: Las Vegas

M. Harrell & Associates
5444 Carolina
Merrillville, IN 46410
219/887-8814
Registration Policy: Submit H/R. Will call if interested.

Affiliates: National and international

Hollywood Look Alikes
3202 N. 1300 E Road
Chebanse, IL 60922
708/848-5755
Registration Policy: Celebrity look-alikes send H/R. Agency will contact if interested.
Audition Policy: Will call if interested.
Affiliate: Marvel Enterprises, LA

Landini Entertainment Productions, Inc.
1029 Donna Lane
Bensenville, IL 60106-2359
630/860-1099
Registration Policy: Specialty talent submit materials to above address.

Live Marketing
1122 N. LaSalle
Chicago, IL 60610
312/787-4800
Nancy Sommers: crowd gatherer
Joe Lauck: presenters/narrators
Registration Policy: Submit H/R. Will call if interested.

Nouvelle Talent
P.O. Box 578100
Chicago, IL 60657
312/944-1133
Equity franchised
Ann Bordalo: television, film, trade show
Carlotta Young: trade show
Registration Policy: Send picture and resumé. (For TV and Film submit photo and resumé to New York office—Nouvelle Talent, 20 Bethune St., Ste 5A, NY, NY 10014.)
Audition Policy: Will contact if interested.
Check In Policy: Phone once a month.
Affiliates: New York

Peter Tye Talent Agency
708/562-5293
Registration Policy: Call for information.

Productions USA
151 N. Michigan, Chicago, IL 60601
312/938-1088
Registration Policy: Send H/R or demo.
Audition Policy: Will call if interested.
Affiliates: NY/LA

Sondra Brewer Trade Shows
1117 Crofton Avenue
Highland Park, IL 60035
847/432-1774
847/432-4909 - fax
Registration Policy: Send H/R. Agency will call if interested. DO NOT CALL.
Audition Policy: Will call for interview/ audition if interested.

Tamar Productions
706 N. Dearborn
Chicago, IL 60610
773/880-1000
Registration Policy: Call for information
Audition Policy: Will ask for promo or materials.
Check In Policy: Every couple of months.

TLW Modeling & Promotions, Inc.
101 W. Grand Avenue #200
Chicago, IL 60610
312/645-0880 • 312/645-0885 - fax
Terri West-Franklin: President
Staci Redisch: new faces, division manager
Registration Policy: 16 and over. New talent should send recent photo and resumé. No open registrations and no drop-ins. Appointments only.
Audition Policy: Agency will call if interested.

Casting Directors

All City Casting
Attn: June Pyskacek
P.O. Box 577640
Chicago, IL 60657-7640
773/588-6062
Type of Work: Union and non-union industrials, films, videos and commercials.
Generals: No.
Submission Policy: Actors may submit H/R by mail. They do keep files of actors' H/Rs. Resubmit only when actor has new pictures, resumé updates, address or phone changes.
Follow-up: NO PHONE CALLS. Updates and invites to shows are welcomed.

Beth Rabedeau Casting
Attn: Beth Rabedeau, Ted Hoerl,
Ken Schoendorf
661 W. Lake
Chicago, IL 60661
312/207-6913 • 312/207-6917 - fax
Type of Work: Both union and non-union.

Mostly commercial, some print and TV.
Generals: Yes. Talent is usually contacted through agents.
Submission Policy: Actors can submit 1 H/R.
Follow-up Policy: Postcards for follow-up and show updates are fine.

Brody, Tenner, Paskal
20 W. Hubbard #2E
Chicago, IL 60610
312/527-0665 • 312/527-9085 - fax
Rachel Tenner: casting director
Mickie Paskal: casting director
Jodi Herrington: casting associate
Type of Work: union - film, TV, commercial
Generals: Occasionally
Submission Policy: Actors can submit 1 H/R.
Follow up Policy: Postcards for follow-up or show updates are fine.

Agencies

CASTING

union & non-union talent

male & female
actors, models, dancers
are needed for
television
productions
& promotions

with a local
broadcast
television
station

send comps
& resume to:

Attn: CASTING
WJYS-TV
18600 S. Oak Park Ave.
Tinley Park, IL 60477

please
NO TELEPHONE CALLS

Communications Corporation of America

Fred Strauss, Executive Producer
2501 N. Sheffield
Chicago, IL 60614
773/348-0001
773/472-7398 - fax

Type of Work: Casts entire productions. Specialized projects.

Submission Policy: Will take submissions through mail. No walk-ins, no calls.

Illinois Film Board member

COMMUNICATIONS CORPORATION OF AMERICA
C A S T I N G
Specializing in teens, pre-teens, and young adults. Major talent break-throughs.
Registered Illinois Film Board.
Award Winning TV Productions.
2501 N. Sheffield
Chicago, IL 60614   **(773) 348.0001**

David O'Connor Casting

Attn: David O'Connor, Scott Nelson
1017 W. Washington #2A
Chicago, IL 60607
312/226-9112

Type of Work: union, non-union - commercial, voice-over, independent film.

Generals: Yes, occasionally.

Submission Policy: 1 H/R

Holly Rick & Heitz Casting

Attn: Rik Kristinat, Holly Womack, Jennifer S. Rudnicke, Hal Watkins
920 N. Franklin #205
Chicago, IL 60610
312/664-0601

Type of Work: union, non-union - commercial, TV, film, print.

Generals: Yes. Monthly on Saturday. This is not a general call. Actor's agent will contact talent if casting director is interested.

Submission Policy: Actors can submit 1 H/R.

Follow-up: Postcards for follow-up and show updates are welcome.

Holzer & Ridge Casting

700 S. Des Plaines
Chicago, IL 60607
312/922-9860

Submission Policy: Women call 312-922-4043; Men call 312-922-4042.

Jane Alderman Casting

Attn: Jane Alderman, Catherine Head, Erica Brown
833 W. Chicago #103
Chicago, IL 60622
312/563-1566 • 312/563-1567 - fax

Type of Work: feature films, television, theatre and commercials.

Non-union work: Only union work, but non-union talent are considered equally if they can join the unions or Taft-Hartley.

Generals: As time permits.

Submission Policy: Actors mail 1 H/R; no tapes unless specifically requested.

Follow-up Policy: BY MAIL ONLY. Invitations to shows and notes regarding recent work are OK.

Kordos & Charbonneau

Attn: Richard Kordos or Nan Charbonneau
P.O. Box 420
Wilmette, IL 60091
847/674-4775

Type of Work: Union - feature film, TV.

Generals: No.

Submission Policy: Actors submit 1 H/R.

Follow-up Policy: Postcards for follow-up and show updates are welcome.

K.T.'s

P.O. Box 577039
Chicago, IL 60657-7039
773/525-1126 • 773/525-1761 - fax

Registration Policy: Send 6 pictures or composites. Include on resumé phone number, address, social security number, height, weight, hair and eye color, age (or age range), car color and make.

Mann-Simon Casting

Attn: Claire Simon
630/653-2922
630/653-1879 - fax

Jean Hetfleisch: office manager

Type of Work: union - TV, film, commercial, industrial.

Generals: Yes

Submission Policy: Receives submissions through agents. Do not submit H/R.

Talking Headshots Casting

Ted Sarantos
2857 N. Halsted
Chicago, IL 60657
773/528-7114
773/528-7153 - fax

Type of Work: union and non-union - commercial, TV, film, some voice-over.

Generals: Yes

Submission Policy: Actors can submit 1 H/R. Will call for general if interested.

Follow-up Policy: Postcards for follow-up and show updates are welcome.

Extras Casting

Casting by McLean/For Extras

P.O. Box #10569
Chicago, IL 60610

Registration Policy: Send headshots and resumés by mail. Include phone number, social security number and all sizes on resumé.

Holzer & Ridge Casting

312/922-4042 - Men
312/922-4043 - Women

Registration Policy: Call for registration info.

K.T.'s

P.O. Box 577039
Chicago, IL 60657-7039
773/525-1126
773/525-1761 - fax

Registration Policy: Send 6 pictures or composites. Include on resumé phone number, address, social security number, height, weight, hair and eye color, age (or age range), car color and make.

Karen Peake Casting

1212 S. Michigan Avenue #1002
Chicago, IL 60605
312/360-9266
312/360-9159 - fax

Registration Policy: Just send SASE. Agency will send registration form.

McCall Model & Talent

6933 S. Crandon #4C
Chicago, IL 60649
773/667-0611
773/667-0636 - fax

Registration Policy: Extras - Appt. only. Send headshot or color snapshot (preferred) and resumé to: Attn: Extras Casting. Include age, height, hair and eye color.

ReginaCast

P.O. Box 585
Willow Springs, IL 60480

Registration Policy: Send a current photo with your age and height, and a 9X12 SASE.

Literary Agents

Austin Wahl Agency
1820 N. 76th Court
Elmwood Park, IL 60070
708/456-2301

Submission Policy: Write letter of interest describing material. Include synopsis, publication history and sample of writing.

International Leonards Corporation
3612 N. Washington Boulevard
Indianapolis, IN 46205
317/926-7566

Submission Policy: Write letter of interest, includeing queries and SASE. Agency will contact if interested. Accepting submissions for TV, Film. NO BOOKS.

Otitis Media Literary Agency
1926 Dupont Avenue South
Minneapolis, MN 55403
612/377-4918

Submission Policy: Write query letter. Include paragraph summary, writing background, and first 20 pages, along with a SASE. Can also email submissions to brbotm19@skypoint.com. NO NEW AGE MATERIAL.

Stewart Talent
58 W. Huron
Chicago, IL 60610
312/943-0892

Submission Policy: Send 2 page synopsis/ summary with SASE to Stewart Talent, Attn: Literary Division. Agency will contact you if interested.

Agencies

A Parents' Guide to Child Acting

I have a daughter (have while she is mine),

Who in her duty and obedience, mark,

Hath given me this.

> **Child Actor:**
> *n.* **1.** a child who is under a minimum legal age employed as a theatrical performer. **2.** a person under the minimum legal age who takes part; a participant.

By Tina O'Brien

Do you want your child to be in the entertainment business?

Before you make that decision, you need to ask yourself a few questions:

- Am I ready for my child to have a career?
- Do I have the time that will be required to help my child succeed?
- If my child does succeed, am I ready to deal with what will happen from there?

If you can honestly answer "yes" to all three questions, then perhaps you and your child are ready to get into this business.

The most important fact about children in the business is that it is a BUSINESS and, like any business, there are **requirements** and **rules of professionalism** that must be met to start your child on the right foot. As a parent, you must be available to take your child on auditions. Many times there is not a whole lot of notice. Generally you will be called for auditions the day before. If you cannot be available, do not waste your time.

The second most important factor is that, if your child is old enough to have an opinion, make sure the child truly is interested. This should not be something that the parent wants more than the child. It should be exciting and fun for all children that are involved.

If you decide you want to proceed with this process, get an agent. When deciding on an agent, make sure that the agencies have children's departments. Agents that have children's departments are listed in this section. Also, ask questions about the agency. Find out about the agency and the agent that is going to be representing your child. This especially holds true if your child is older and is embarking on a television and film career.

Most agencies require you to send in pictures of your child. The pictures can be professional or snapshots. If you are submitting snapshots, make sure to have on the back of the photo: your child's name, date of birth, height, weight and date of the picture.

Most agencies require you to send in a self-addressed stamped envelope in order for you to receive a response either way or to return the pictures if they are not interested. Please make sure that you include an envelope that is big enough to fit the pictures. You can usually allow 4 to 6 weeks for the process to be complete.

When you call an agency, to get the best response, make sure that you have your questions written down, and be brief and to the point. Agents do not make money until the child makes money. Agencies work on commission. There should be no registration fees of any sort! I have heard that some people are required to go to a seminar for which you have to pay a fee. Please research that before you do it. I would never require someone to pay money to go to a seminar before I register him or her.

If an agency accepts your child, it is not guaranteeing work. This business is very unpredictable. Be patient and hope for the best.

If you choose to get professional pictures before you submit to the agencies, there is a list of photographers in this book. When choosing a photographer, make sure the photographer really likes working with

Kids

children. It is definitely acceptable to ask to see some of their work. If a child is not comfortable with the photographer, it will definitely show in the pictures. Many people wait to get an agent before they have professional pictures done. Either way is acceptable.

There are several areas in which you can get involved in the business. Your child can be involved in print modeling, commercials, television or film. Some children excel in one area more than others. As you learn more about the business, you will begin to see which areas your child may be right for. For print work, looks are important, as well as size and teeth. For commercials, it is important that your child be outgoing and have lots of personality.

Going through the process of getting your child in the business, you will undoubtedly run in to insider terminology. Here are some definitions of general terms which may help you in the very beginning.

Look-See Casting: Usually used when referring to a print audition. You will bring your child to the photographer/client and they will either just look at your child or take a Polaroid.

Audition: Going to the client or agent and "trying out" for a role in a commercial, film, etc. This can consist of a quick interview, or may possibly require your child to memorize a script. This will depend on the type of audition.

Composite: Several pictures of your child that are on one professionally 8 x 10 printed sheet. It also will have the child's statistics — height, weight, age range — printed on it as well. This is used for modeling.

Headshot: This is one picture that is used for on-camera work.

The best advice I can give to a parent just getting started is to do your research, be professional, be prepared. Always have a map with you. Always be on time (not too early and definitely not late) and make this fun for your child. Read through other parts of this book. Advice given to grown-up actors is just as useful for child actors. This business can be a very positive and rewarding experience for your child if handled correctly by the parents. Good luck!

Kids' Training

ALYO Children's Dance Theatre
7825 S. Elllis Avenue
Chicago, IL 60619
773/723-2596 • 773/723-2396 - fax

Beverly Art Center
2153 W. 111th Street
Chicago, IL 60643
773/445-3838

Dance: Tap, Modern, Ballet, Jazz

BizKids
P.O. Box 211
Flossmoor, IL 60422-0211
708/799-2808 • 800/569-1022

BizKids practically supports the show biz parent and their young performer via workshops, a quarterly newsletter, on-camera acting/audition classes, fun and educational resources and a parent mentoring network.

Chicago Academy for the Arts
1010 W. Chicago Avenue
Chicago, IL 60622
312/421-0202

A high school specializing in training for the performing arts.

Dance: Modern, Jazz, Ballet

Chicago Ballet Arts
Claire Carmichael - Director
7416 N. Ridge
Chicago, IL 60645
773/381-0000 • 847/657-8121 - fax

Ballet: Children to 18 years, beginning to pre-professional

DancEd
3131 Dundee Road
Northbrook, IL 60062
847/564-9120

Dance: Ballet, Tap, Jazz, Hip Hop

DancInc
Nutrier West Center
7 Happ Road
Northfield, IL 60093
847/501-2024

Storybook Dance + Drama for Children (ages 2 1/2 - 6)
Summer Performing Arts Camp (ages 4-10)

DePaul University - Community Music Division
804 W. Belden Avenue
Chicago, IL 60614-3296
773/325-7000 • 773/325-7264 - fax

DEPAUL COMMUNITY MUSIC

MUSICAL THEATER WORKSHOP
Grades 7-12
Acting • Movement • Vocal Techniques

For information, call (773) 325-7262

ETA Creative Arts
7558 S. Chicago Avenue
Chicago, IL 60619
773/752-3955

Eileen Boevers Performing Arts Workshop
595 Elm Place
Highland Park, IL 60035
847/432-4335

The Eileen Boevers Performing Arts Workshop, now in its 27th year, offers professional arts instruction in a supportive environment for ages 4 through adult. With locations throughout the North Shore suburban area, classes include drama, dance, musical comedy, voice, improvisation, stage stunts and combination classes. Call for complete workshop information.

Fieldcrest School
of Performing Arts
11639 S. Ashland
Chicago, IL 60643
773/568-6706

Dance: Ballet, Tap, Jazz, Modern

Moravec
847/733-9801

New American Theatre
118 N. Main
Rockford, IL 61101
815/963-9454
815/963-7215 - fax

Discovering Drama (Ages 5-7)
Story Theater (Ages 8-10)
You're On! (Ages 11-13)
Scene Study (Ages 14-18)
Shakespeare (Ages 16+)

Piven Theatre Workshop
927 Noyes #102
Evanston, IL 60201
847/866-6597 • 847/866-6614 - fax
Grades 4-6
Theatre Games & Story Theatre
Advanced Theatre Games & Story Theatre
Grades 7-8
Theatre Games & Story Theatre
Advanced Theatre Games & Story Theatre
Introductory Scene Study
High School
Theatre Games & Story Theatre
Advanced Theatre Games & Story Theatre
Scene Study
Advanced Scene Study

Young Actor's Program
Administrative Offices
872 W. Buckingham
Chicago, IL 60657
773/883-0846

Talent Agencies - Kids

Many agencies handle child talent. The following are those agencies who list an agent specifically for kids. See the listings in chapter 2 for more details on particular agencies.

Arlene Wilson Models
430 W. Erie #210
Chicago, IL 60610
312/573-0200
312/573-0046 - fax
AFTRA/SAG/Equity franchised
Contact: Laura Alexander, Lisa Goren

CED (Cunningham, Escott, DiPene)
1 E. Superior Street #505
Chicago, IL 60611
312/944-5600

312/944-9746 - VO
312/944-5694 - fax
SAG/AFTRA/Equity franchised
Contact: Monica Valdean - Tina O'Brien

Harrise Davidson & Associates
65 E. Wacker Place #2401
Chicago, IL 60601
312/782-4480
312/782-3363 - fax
AFTRA/SAG/Equity franchised
Contact: Jen Barnett

Stewart Talent
58 W. Huron
Chicago, IL 60610
312/943-3131
312/943-2590 - fax
AFTRA/SAG/Equity franchised
Contact: Kathi Gardner,
Elizabeth Oldroyd, Sheila Dougherty

Suzanne's A-Plus
108 W. Oak
Chicago, IL 60610
312/642-8151
312/943-9751 - fax
AFTRA/SAG/WGA franchised
Contact: Marsha Becker

Kids' Theatres

Evanston Youth Theatre
Workshop Program
2010 Dewey Avenue
Evanston, IL 60201
847/328-5740

Kids

Unions and
Organizations

A long with talent agencies, unions are the most confusing parts of a performing career. If you want to make a consistent living in this business, though, you're going to have to deal with them sooner or later. Hopefully, in the following pages we have made the unions a bit more accessible.

Actors Equity Association

Good my lord, will you see the players well bestowed? Do you hear? Let them be well used, for they are the abstract and brief chronicles of the time. After your death you were better have a bad epitaph than their ill report while you live.

By Carrie L. Kaufman

If you're at all familiar with theatre on the coasts, you know that getting your Equity card is the first and foremost priority on young actors' minds. People do summer theatre as much for the Equity points as for the experience. They will find anything to get that Equity card.

Not in Chicago.

Non-Equity theatre rules in Chicago. There are, at any given time, over 200 theatres in this city and only 41 were Equity in 1997. Of those, 16-18 were Tier N, which is, for all intents and purposes, the stage between Equity and non-Equity.

This is not to say that actors can't, or shouldn't, join **Actors Equity Association**. But you must be wise about where your career is going and if you are ready to make the commitment. Once you join, you cannot do non-Equity theatre again unless you drop out of the union, forfeiting your dues and entrance fee and any benefits you may have accrued.

"It's a decision that people need to be prepared for and not have it 'happen' to them," says Kathryn Lamke, executive director of the central region of AEA.

Actors need to consider the types of roles they can realistically be cast in. If you're a quirky, specialty character type, would it be wise to take that Goodman Equity contract and shut off the few future roles available by closing the non-Equity door? On the other hand, are there millions of people just like you who could be offered a non-Equity contract for less money in an Equity show and still be available to do non-Equity theatre?

"In the younger performer — or someone who plays young — if there are other performers of equal ability out there...you don't have as much leverage as someone who is 45 and knows very well that there aren't that many good 45-year-old non-Equity actors" who haven't dropped out of the business, Lamke says.

Let's say you're a 25-year-old, non-Equity actress in the Equity Membership Candidate Program who has accumulated almost enough points to join the union. The next job in an Equity theatre will put you over the top. But you've been working steadily in the non-Equity theatre company you formed with friends a few years ago. Then Steppenwolf wants to cast you. It will fulfill your dream, but keep you off your own stage. And there's no guarantee that the next Equity show with a role for your type won't go to the one of the thousands of other 25-year-old actresses in Chicago. What do you do?

"They may need to say no to Steppenwolf," says Lamke. "That's the conversation they need to have with themselves before they audition."

While you're talking to yourself, consider this: In the last decade Actors Equity in Chicago has bent over backwards to embrace small theatre companies, giving their members many more opportunities to work. The Chicago Area Theatre (CAT) contract has seven tiers with, among other things, different salary structures and casting requirements. Most exciting is the Tier N contract, which has made it possible for small, low-budget theatres to hire Equity actors on a show-by-show basis. (See below for a complete rundown of Equity contracts frequently used in the Chicago area.)

Lamke says she is gratified to know that "our relationship with theatres is not really a philosophical issue, it's an economic issue. They like what we do; they just don't have the money." Tier N has done a great deal to make the economics less of an issue.

By the way, for those lucky enough to be considering whether or not to turn down that Steppenwolf job, Lamke has a cogent reminder: "If you're truly good enough, they are going to take you the next time."

Membership

There are three ways to join Actors Equity Association:

1) Get cast in an Equity show and sign an Equity contract.

2) Be a member in good standing of one of the eight unions that make up the 4-A's (Associated Actors and Artists of America). The sister unions are: AFTRA (the American Federation of Television and Radio Artists), SAG (the Screen Actors Guild), AGMA (the American Guild of Musical Artists), AGVA (the American Guild of Variety Artists), SEG (Screen Extras Guild), HAU (the Hebrew Actors Union), APATE (Association of Puerto Rican Artists and Theatrical Employees) and IAG (the International Artists Guild).

3) Join the Equity Membership Candidate Program.

The first avenue is possible, but rare.

The second is up to the other unions.

The **Equity Membership Candidate Program** (EMC) gives non-Equity actors the chance to work in Equity theatres and earn points toward Equity membership. The first step is getting cast for a non-Equity role by an Equity theatre who participates in the program. That's where summer theatre comes in.

Once you enroll and pay your $100 fee (which will go toward your initiation fee once you join the union), you can audition for a non-union slot in any Equity show; though, as of 1997, you no longer get to audition with Equity actors. You earn points for each week you work in an Equity show until you reach 50 weeks, when you can join the union. At that point, you cannot be hired by an Equity theatre unless they sign you to an Equity contract.

The **initiation fee** for joining Actors Equity Association is $800 as of early 1998. Members also must pay **semi-annual dues** totaling $78 and pay 2 percent of their gross salary for each Equity contract they sign.

Once you join Actors Equity, be aware that you might have to change your name. The only places two people can't have the same name are in soap operas and actors' unions. Some people use all three of their names (John Godfrey Smith), some just drop the last name (John Godfrey), while some use their middle initial (Michael J. Fox). Then again, some people completely reinvent their identities.

Unions & Organizations

Benefits

Equity members have access to a **health plan**, a **vision care plan** and, coming this summer, a **dental plan**. Equity currently has two health insurance plans available in Chicago: a Blue Cross/Blue Shield basic plan and MaxiCare HMO.

Equity actors can be eligible for one year of health benefits if they complete 10 Equity work weeks in a 12-month period. They have to keep working 10 weeks or more to maintain health benefits.

Other benefits are a bit less tangible, but make up the backbone of Equity's existence. For instance, all producers must post a **bond** for each show, so Equity members can get paid if the show closes early. The union also administers a **pension plan** and provides **workman's compensation**. Actors under Equity contracts must be given certain breaks at certain periods of time, and the work space must be of a certain standard. Actors also can't work more than so many hours in a day or week and you must be fed timely and properly. If you supply a costume piece, you must, under Equity rules, be paid rental for that costume by the theatre.

I could go on. It's a union.

Contracts

Equity theatres in the Chicago area work under four basic types of contracts: **CAT** (Chicago Area Theatre), **LORT** (League of Resident Theatres), **Dinner Theatre** and **Children's Theatre**. There are 27 different contracts for Actors Equity around the country and many more than four in Chicago. But these are the ones Chicago actors will be most likely to run into.

CAT

The Chicago Area Theatre contract came to being in the mid-1980's as a more flexible alternative to other Equity contracts. It is divided into seven tiers which specify, among other things, different salary arrangements and shows per week. Each tier has a standard minimum salary and benefits, but often theatres negotiate their own. Every tier but Tier N requires at least one Equity actor plus an Equity stage manager. Tier N requires the stage manager be an Equity Membership Candidate. All Tiers II - VI require understudies, though the understudies do not have to be Equity members. An Equity understudy who is required to be there all the time would be paid the same as an Equity actor. An understudy who is hired on a "stand-by" basis would be paid a salary equivalent to three tiers down from the tier the show is working under. For instance, a stand-by understudy for a Tier VI theatre would be paid a Tier III salary, which would go up when the understudy went on. CAT theatres can be for-profit or non-profit.

Here is a brief rundown of the CAT tiers:

Tier VI: Up to eight performances a week with a salary range of $535.25 to $639 a week.

Tier V: Up to eight performances a week with a salary range of $446.50 to $522 a week.

Tier IV: Up to seven performances a week with a salary range of $378.75 to $433.50 a week.

Tier III: Up to six performances a week with a salary range of $266.50 to $309 a week.

Tier II: Up to five performances a week with a salary range of $196.25 to $225.25 a week.

Tier I: Up to four performances a week with a salary range of $130 to $157.75 a week.

Tier N: Up to four performances a week with a salary range of $129 to $150, with no requirement to hire an Equity stage manager or understudies or contribute to the health insurance fund. In addition, Tier N theatres must do 50 percent of their season as Equity shows. Tier N work weeks do not count towards an actor's eligibility for health care benefits.

In addition, CAT contracts offer a **"More Renumerative Employment"** clause. Essentially, if an actor gets a higher paying job — say a national commercial — then the theatre is required to let the actor do the commercial and put on an understudy in his or her stead until the job ends. This was a recognition that actors in Chicago earn their bread and butter from on-camera work and that, if theatres wanted to attract actors who might earn more, they needed to promise them time off when the opportunities came up. The MRE is applicable to all CAT contracts, including CAT N. It is not applicable to many other Equity contracts. LORT and Dinner Theatre contracts, for instance, don't have MRE's.

LORT

The **League of Resident Theatres** is a membership organization of non-profit regional theatres around the U.S. Guthrie is LORT. Arena Stage is LORT. Basically, the anchor regional theatre in any city is probably a

Unions & Organizations

member of LORT and, therefore, under a LORT Equity contract. Advantages of being a LORT theatre are that all union contracts are negotiated nationally by representatives of LORT and the organization is recognized by funders. LORT contracts with Equity permit touring and cover musical and non-musical theatre. Salary and contract requirements are based on the theatre's budget and box office grosses. There are five levels: A, B+, B, C & D. Theatres may employ a resident company, but are not required to do so.

Chicago has two LORT contract theatres: **Goodman** and **Northlight.** The Goodman mainstage is under a LORT B+ contract, which pays a minimum of $619 a week. Northlight and the Goodman Studio are under a LORT D contract, which pays $459 a week.

Dinner Theatre

Chicago is the birthplace of dinner theatre. Over 35 years ago, William Pullinsi took some inheritance money and started Candlelight Dinner Playhouse, inventing the concept of dinner theatre. Candlelight, sadly, closed its doors last year, but the concept lives on all over the country. Most of the dinner theatres in the Chicago area are in the suburbs, and most focus their attention on musical theatre. Happy is easier to digest. There are six tier structures under the Dinner Theatre contract. Salary is based on seating capacity. Actors Equity must approve any dinner theatre in Chicago (and New York City, Los Angeles County or San Francisco). Dinner does not have to be served in the same room as the show. This puts theatres such as **Marriott's Lincolnshire** — which often sells restaurant/theatre packages — under this contract. Both Marriott's and **Drury Lane Oakbrook Terrace** are under Tier VI contracts. **Drury Lane Evergreen Park** is under a Tier IV contract. Salary ranges are currently in negotiation and were not available at press time.

Theatre for Young Audiences

TYA is the contract for children's theatre in Chicago. Actors can be hired on a weekly contract or a per-performance contract. Performances generally don't begin after 7 p.m. and may not exceed 90 minutes in length. The contract allows for "associated artist activity," such as classes and workshops with students. Both local and overnight touring are permitted. This contract is used both for resident companies who have an outreach program and for companies that make their livings touring schools. Actors can make decent supplementary income doing children's theatre in Chicago.

AFTRA & SAG

Actors can get pretty steady work in commercials, industrials, voice-overs and film in Chicago. Most of it's paid. Some of it's paid well. Almost all of it's union.

The **American Federation of Television and Radio Artists (AFTRA)** and the **Screen Actors Guild (SAG)** are the two performer unions. They are closely related. In fact, they may merge in the fall of 1998. In Chicago, AFTRA and SAG are run out of the same office under one executive director. They are, like all unions, run by an elected board of members.

Whether or not a production is covered by AFTRA or SAG is quite complicated, and is one of the reasons union members have been clamoring for a merger for decades.

SAG covers all **movies** and all **animation**, regardless of the medium. If a movie is shot on film, it's SAG. If it's shot on digital video, it's still SAG. It's SAG even if it's only released on TV.

AFTRA covers **radio** and **vocal recording**, as well as **broadcast news**. It also covers **awards shows** and **soap operas.**

Union jurisdiction gets murky when it comes to commercials, industrials (work-place videos), basic cable and non-prime-time programming or syndicated programming. Officially, it's up to the producer to decide which contract to use. In cities where AFTRA and SAG are administered out of the same office, jurisdiction over television commercials and industrials is determined by the medium used. Commercials and industrials in Chicago, for instance, are SAG if they are shot on film and AFTRA if they are shot on video.

"It can be confusing," says Kit Woods, assistant executive director of AFTRA and SAG in Chicago. "When you administer both contracts, you have to find a way to make it work."

Unions & Organizations

Membership

Joining AFTRA and SAG is fairly easy, though not cheap. You can join AFTRA at any time by simply paying the initiation fee and half a year's dues. For SAG, you first have to get cast under a SAG contract. That means you land your first big commercial (for convenience sake, let's say it's shot on film and is SAG), or even local SAG commercial, or you get the role of the young doctor who comes into the hospital room and says, "It's late. Everybody out," in the latest Bruce Willis flick. Once you get that contract, you are eligible to join SAG. But you don't have to join right away.

As you're signing that contract, you will likely hear — from your agent or the casting director, or even the production coordinator — two words: **Taft-Hartley**. "You're Taft-Hartley now, so you'd better call the union," the production coordinator will say as she bumps you up from an extra to a speaking role. You reach into memories of your high school history class and vaguely remember something called the Taft-Hartley Act. But what does that have to do with a movie about Babe Ruth?

The **Taft-Hartley Act** is one of the laws that covers unions and is also known as the National Labor Relations Act. Essentially, it says that a union can't require somebody to join until 30 days after their first day of employment. For a steel worker, that's a month after they're hired. For an actor, that could be years after they get their first job.

Say you get bumped up from one of the extras sitting in the stands at Wrigley Field to the part of a reporter shouting questions at the Babe as he stomps off. You may be on a roll and your agent may call you in for another speaking role in a SAG commercial or film a few days later and you land that role, which starts shooting two weeks after you got the first role. It's been less than 30 days since you signed your first SAG contract, so you don't have to join the union, even for that second job. If you get a third SAG job within 30 days of getting the first, you don't have to join SAG for that either. Congratulations, you've just had a very rare, busy and lucrative month.

Then your luck runs out and you don't get cast for any SAG jobs for two years, when you land a role in John McNaughton's next film. Because 30 days have passed since your first SAG contract role in the Babe movie, you automatically have to join SAG. This has to happen before you even start shooting. The production company will fax a cast list to SAG and they will check that list against their databases. Your name will come up and they will make you fork over the appropriate fees immediately.

This is when actors get in trouble. **The initiation fee for SAG is currently $1,118.** That number is the equivalent of two day-rates in a theatrical film or television show. Minimum yearly dues are $85, to be paid in twice-yearly installments — the first in addition to the initiation fee when you join. **The initiation fee for AFTRA is currently $1,000.** Minimum yearly dues are $113, to be paid in twice-yearly installments. Dues for both unions are based on an actor's earnings.

So, you've spent all the money you made two years ago doing SAG jobs under the Taft-Hartley 30-day protection. Now you have to fork over $1,122.50 to the union *before you even step on the set.* Don't have it? Too bad. You should have put it away two years ago in anticipation of having to join.

Sometimes people who have no intention of doing SAG work just fall into it. I actually got a call in 1991 from a guy who had been bumped to a principal from an extra slot during the filming of *A League of Their Own.* Mostly, it takes a lot of hard work and frustrating rejections before an actor gets to that point. You would think, then, that actor would know all the business stuff and not be surprised when the union came knocking. Depressingly, this is not always the case.

If Woods could just say one thing to actors, it would be this: "If you've decided that you want to go compete for professional work, then you really need to get your act together to investigate it." If you get hired under a SAG or AFTRA contract, call the office and ask them what you should do.

Contracts

There are multiple SAG and AFTRA contracts for various aspects of the business. I am not going to list them here. Under some contracts, you might just get paid a session fee. Under others, you might get paid a session fee plus residuals, with more to be negotiated after the sale of the production. SAG and AFTRA have books on this.

By way of example, let's look at what might happen if an actor gets cast in a national commercial under an AFTRA or SAG contract. A national commercial session fee is $478.70, which includes the shoot and the first time the commercial runs. If the commercial only runs once — even if it's in the Super Bowl — the actor gets paid $478.70.

Commercials run on 13-week cycles. If the commercial goes out on a network feed and runs multiple times a day — such as that smiling Nissan guy (and his little dog, too) — the actors in it get paid each time it runs. In addition to the session and first run fee, the actors get paid $122.70 for the second run of the commercial, $97.35 for the 3rd through 13th runs, and $46.65 for each run after that.

After 13 weeks, the ad agency may elect to drop the commercial, keep the commercial running (sometimes edited differently) or reshoot it with the same actors. If they reshoot it with the same actors, you're agent will probably negotiate a better fee. If the same commercial gets picked up for another 13 weeks, the entire cycle starts over again, starting with the $478.70 for the first run. This can be quite lucrative.

For basic cable, the actors in the commercial get paid a maximum lump sum of $1,014 for 13 weeks *no matter how many times the commercial runs.* So next time your see that Nissan guy and think he's getting paid a bundle, note whether or not you're watching network or cable TV. He might not be getting as much as you think.

Product Conflict

If the ad agency decides to not run the commercial, they still might have to pay you. Under rules governing **product conflict,** an actor under contract to do a commercial for one type of product — such as a Nissan — cannot turn around and do a commercial for a competitive product — such as the Ford F150. Remember, image is everything, and neither ad agencies nor their clients want that cuddly yet enigmatic man the public is so identifying with to show up selling a competitive product.

"Exclusivity is a big deal," says Woods. "The advertisers demand it." In that case, the advertiser must pay the actor a holding fee to keep the actor from being in a competitive commercial. The **holding fee,** paid every 13 weeks, is equivalent to the session fee, or $478.70 in this case. For nice, national campaigns, the agency and client might pay the fee for a few years. That's an extra couple of thousand in your pocket for work you did long ago.

Now, suppose you did a non-union commercial for MaidRite hamburgers back in your hometown of Waterloo, Iowa in the summer of 1990. Then you get cast in a national Burger King commercial. Great, right? Sorry. You are quite out of luck. The MaidRite commercial was non-union, so product conflict is permanent. The MaidRite people may still be running the commercial. If not, they don't have to pay you anything to hold the commercial, and they can run it any time. In fact, if the owner of the store sees your face coming across his TV screen every hour or so, he might decide to take your old commercial out of the can and exploit your newfound familiarity.

In short, if you make a non-union commercial, you can never do a union commercial for the same type of product. Period. You may, if you want to pay the legal bills, go back and draw up a contract with the non-union client to not use the commercial again. You may have to pay the non-union client a hefty sum in order to do so.

If you ignore that MaidRite commercial and take the Burger King job, then someone from Burger King notices your younger face on a local TV station in Iowa, the trouble you can get into is enormous. The production company may simply be able to cut you out of the Burger King commercial, and you'll have to forfeit any fees you may have earned. If they can't do that, and the Burger King bigwigs and the ad agency decide to pull the commercial, *you could be liable for all of the expenses incurred to put that commercial together.* Everything. The entire production — hundreds of thousands of dollars — could be charged to you.

Similar consequences can ensue if you did a union commercial for McDonald's in 1990 and have simply "forgotten" about those checks McDonald's is still paying you in holding fees. In 20 years with the union, Kit Woods has only seen this happen twice. Both were settled by cutting the actor out. They were lucky. That said, if you do a union commercial for McDonald's and they stop paying you holding fees, they cannot run that commercial again without hiring you again. Then you are free to do the Burger King commercial.

Benefits

AFTRA and SAG are unions and give their members the same benefits as any union, including pension and retirement and health plans. Actors must earn $7,500 in a 12-month period to get one year of health insurance. To

Unions & Organizations

keep it, they have to make at least $7,500 a year.

On set, AFTRA and SAG negotiate everything from meals and bathroom breaks to overtime. There are myriad rules, and it would behoove any actor to call the AFTRA/SAG office to find out what they are. "Personally," says Woods, "I want the performers to learn their business, to understand the basic provisions in their contracts, because they often get cheated."

If an actor is on a shoot and something comes up that is questionable — say the production manager says everybody is working overtime and not getting paid overtime rates — Woods advises actors to stay cool. Tell the production manager that it's all right with you if it's all right with your union and your agent, then get on the horn and call either one. Let them do the arguing for you.

Joining a union is never an easy process. There are rules and regulations galore. Sometimes it might seem as if they get in the way. But all the rules are there to protect the members. And actors need all the protection they can get.

Unions

Actors Equity Association
203 N. Wabash #170
Chicago, IL 60601
312/641-0393
312/641-6365 - fax

**American Federation of TV &
Radio Artists (AFTRA)**
1 E. Erie #650
Chicago, IL 60611
312/573-8081
312/573-0318 - fax

Chicago Dance Coalition
200 N. Michigan #404
Chicago, IL 60601
312/419-8384
312/419-0603 - fax

**Chicago Federation of Musicians
Local 10 208 AFM**
175 W. Washington
Chicago, IL 60602
312/782-0063
312/782-7880 - fax

Directors Guild of America
400 N. Michigan #307
Chicago, IL 60611
312/644-5050
312/644-5776 - fax

Screen Actors Guild (SAG)
1 E. Erie #650
Chicago, IL 60611
312/573-8081
312/573-0318 - fax

Actors Don't Have to be Victims

Where to go when you have been pushed too far.

Resource:
n. **1.** a source of supply, support or aid, esp. one held in reserve. **2.** the quality of being resourceful

By Carrie L. Kaufman

Acting is a brutal business. Teachers and casting directors will tell you that actors have to be in control of what they can control and let go of the rest. This is good advice. The reason it's given is that there is very little actors can control.

Still, **actors don't have to be victims.** You should be treated with the respect with which any professional treats a fellow professional. You should also, of course, give that respect and act professionally. But when the line is crossed, actors don't have to sit there and take it.

Where that line is drawn is up to you. You must decide what you're willing to take and when you're willing to fight back. There is no global answer. You must decide on a case-by-case basis.

Say, for instance, you send your headshot and resume with a cover letter and self addressed stamped envelope to a SAG franchised agent. Then a week later you get it all back with a line through your cover letter and the words "not interested" written over the type. What do you do? It's not really something SAG or AFTRA can do anything about. They can and will be sympathetic, but that's about all. This might be a case in which you slough if off to the indignities actors must deal with.

You might make a copy and stick it in an envelope addressed to the head of the agency, with a nice letter informing her that someone in her office probably had a very bad day.

If it's a reputable agent, he or she should be as horrified by that kind of treatment as you. By the way, this actually happened to one of the people working on this book. Recently. At a very reputable agency.

If, however, you are called into an agent's office and told that you really need to have pictures done in the nude and he happens to be a photographer on the side, leave immediately and call SAG or AFTRA or one of the agencies listed below.

Basically, if alarm bells go off in your head, it's for a reason. If you've only suffered a rudeness, the people listed below will be sympathetic and tell you they can't help you. If you've suffered more, they will tell you that too and help you redress the situation.

Unions

Unions are there to protect members from all sorts of indignities, from pay disputes to harassment. If you are a member of AFTRA, SAG or Actors Equity Association, call them. Even if you're not a member, call them. Your complaint might fall under their jurisdiction. If not, they can help you get to the proper agency.

If you walk into a casting director's office and he or she makes a lewd remark about you or asks you to take off your shirt for the audition, call your union and your agent. Don't assume that you're being too sensitive. Sometimes there are legitimate reasons for this (such as soap commercials), but those instances are very rare.

In any case, if auditioning nude is legitimate, your agent will be notified and you will have that information before you even accept the audition. There will also be all sorts of precautions, such as only necessary personnel in the room, including at least one other woman (if you're a woman). There should be no surprises.

SAG also can help if your agent hasn't paid you in a timely fashion, or if she takes out more than 10 percent from your pay. Usually, this happens with non-union franchised agents, but SAG can point you in the right direction to file a complaint.

Employment Issues
Illinois Department of Labor
160 N. LaSalle - 13th Floor
Chicago, IL 60601
Joyce Markmann (agent questions)
Phone: 312/793-1817
Wage Claim Division (for employment compensation)
Phone: 312/793-2808

The Department of Labor is the agency that handles disputes between employers and employees — or their agents.

There are two basic divisions in the Department of Labor that actors need to know about. The first is Joyce Markmann's division.

Remember that name. If you've been wronged and you need an ally, call **Joyce Markmann.** She is a down-to-earth, no-nonsense woman who has a passion for getting people who take advantage of other people. She is the best friend an actor has in state government.

Markmann deals with problems with agencies — even bogus ones. If your agent starts taking 20 percent out of your check, call Joyce. She'll look up their file and tell you what they've told the state they charge in commission. If it's only 10 percent, she'll get in touch with the agent and get them to pay you the other 10 percent. She also might start disciplinary action if she gets too many complaints.

The same is true for agents who pay slowly or not at all. Say you did a commercial months ago and still haven't gotten paid. You call your agent, and they tell you the client hasn't paid them. Then you run into someone who was on that same commercial — booked through another agency — and they tell you they got paid over a month ago. Call Joyce Markmann.

Especially call Joyce if you run into an agent who doesn't seem to be licensed. Markmann is full of stories about people who have been taken advantage of. Stories about so-called "agents" calling young mothers in by telling them their kid is just perfect for modeling or commercials, then charging them $800 to take the kid's picture or video tape — and telling them they have to come back in six months to do the same thing

Unions & Organizations

because the kid has grown. Nothing ever happens to the headshot or video tape. The kid is never sent out on any jobs. And even if he was sent out, the mother still needn't have paid. Agents get paid by the client after they get you the job. **Actors should never pay to get a job.**

Markmann recently helped police arrest some child pornographers in Buffalo Grove from an audition notice she spotted that sounded fishy. Turns out the police were already watching the house.

"My little contribution sometimes gets the ball rolling," Markmann says.

If your dispute is directly with an employer and it deals with your pay, call the **Wage Claim Division** of the Department of Labor. They step in when an actor is paid less than they were hired for or when an actor is not paid at all (if, in fact, the theatre or production company has agreed to pay in the first place).

If you feel you've been wronged in your pay, file a complaint with the Wage Claim Division. They will send a letter to the employer. When they get the employer's response, they will compare your claim to their response and either dismiss it or send it to the next level, which is a hearing. If the employer is found liable in the hearing, he or she has a certain amount of time to pay. If the employer still doesn't pay, Wage Claim then sends it to the Attorney General's office, where legal proceedings are begun. For this last phase to take place, actors need to stay in touch with the Department of Labor after an employer is found liable. The department has no way knowing if the employer has fulfilled his or her obligations unless you tell them.

The Equal Opportunity Employment Commission

National Office
1801 L Street, N.W.
Washington, D.C. 20507
Phone: 202/663-4900
TDD: 202/663-4494
Web: http://www.eeoc.gov

Chicago District Office
500 West Madison Street
Suite 2800
Chicago, IL 60661
Phone: 312/353-2713
TDD: 312/353-242

The **EEOC** protects against discrimination in the workplace. If you feel you've been sexually harassed, call the EEOC and make a complaint. If you feel you've been dismissed because of your race, call the EEOC.

There are laws that protect you, and the commission will check out your story. Chances are, you aren't the only one who has complained.

In cases of sexual discrimination — including harassment and pregnancy — you can also call the **Women's Bureau,** which has regional offices all over the country. The Chicago office of the Women's Bureau is at 312/353-6985. They cover the Illinois, Indiana, Michigan, Minnesota, Ohio and Wisconsin areas.

The Women's Bureau is not an enforcing agency. They are a resource for information and statistics on women in the workplace. But they can give you advice or point you in the right direction if you feel you've been wronged.

Department of Human Rights
100 W. Randolph, Suite 10-100
Chicago, IL 60601
Phone: 312/814-6200
Web: http://www.state.il.us.dhr

The Illinois Department of Human Rights deals with any sort of discrimination in the work force. They are essentially the state alternative to the EEOC. If you've been fired because you're pregnant, call them. If you've been fired because you're over 40, they can help. If you've been fired — or not hired — because you're African-American or Hispanic or have an unfavorable military discharge or arrest record, call them.

They are also the place to call if you've been the victim of sexual harassment.

If you feel you've been discriminated against, call the Department of Human Rights. You will need to go there and file a complaint, which consists of filling out a four-page form and going through an interview. Plan to spend half a day there.

After your complaint is filed, the employer will be notified and given time to respond. In the meantime, the Department of Human Rights, with your help, will try to find other people who may have gone through the same things you have, in order to build a stronger case.

After the employer responds, you and the employer are brought into the

Unions & Organizations

same room for a fact-finding conference. Then everything is turned over
to the Department. of Human Rights' legal department. If they find
"substantial evidence" that discrimination has occurred, they will send it
over to the Human Rights Commission, which takes legal action.

Consumer Issues

Illinois Attorney General
100 W. Randolph
Chicago, IL 60601
General Information: 312/814-3000
(Check the white pages for specific departments.)

The Office of the Attorney General deals with consumer issues. If a
long distance telephone company takes over your service without your
knowledge or consent (in other words, if you get "slammed"), file a
complaint with the Attorney General's office. If you pay to get your
headshots reproduced and the company goes bankrupt after it's cashed
your check, call the Attorney General's office.

The Attorney General also will go after an employer who has not paid
an employee and has been found liable by the Illinois Department of
Labor (see above).

Better Business Bureau
Chicago Office
330 N. Wabash
Chicago, IL 60611
Phone: 312/832-0500

The Better Business Bureau deals with contracts and obligations. If you
purchased a computer from a mail-order house in California and your
credit card has been charged but you haven't gotten the computer and
the seller says they've never heard of you, call the Better Business
Bureau. If you paid a photographer to take your headshot but the film
came out totally black and he won't give you your money back, call the
Better Business Bureau (as well as the Attorney General's office, in
both cases.)

If, however, that same photographer asks you to pose nude or if an agent starts yelling and screaming obscenities at you, the Better Business Bureau will be of no help. They may be sympathetic, but they do not deal with matters of behavior. If you paid for a product or service and received that product or service, or if you received a refund if the product was defective or the service not provided, the Better Business Bureau is completely satisfied.

Other Helpful Organizations

Arts and Business Council of Chicago
70 E. Lake #500
Chicago, IL 60601
312/372-1876

Chicago Film Office
1 N. LaSalle #2165
Chicago, IL 60602
312/744-6415
312/744-1378

Illinois Arts Alliance
200 N. Michigan #404
Chicago, IL 60601
312/855-3105
312/855-1565 - fax

Illinois Arts Council
100 W. Randolph #10 500
Chicago, IL 60601
312/814-6750

League of Chicago Theatres
67 E. Madison #2116
Chicago, IL 60603
312/977-1730
900/225-2225

The League promotes Chicago's theatre industry through marketing, advocacy, and information services. Programs include Hot Tix, Chicago Theater Guide, Play Money, Gift Certificates, and Theater Info Line. The League coordinates the annual Non-Traditional Auditions for seniors and persons of color or with disabilities, and the Non-Equity General Auditions in May and June. The annual retreat, with industry-related workshops and seminars open to the public, will be held on August 14-15, 1998.

National Dinner Theatre Association
P.O. Box 726
Marshall, MI 49068
616/781-7859
616/781-4880 - fax

Women in the Directors Chair
3435 N. Sheffield #202
Chicago, IL 60657
773/281-4988
773/281-4999 - fax

Unions & Organizations

Theatres

At any given time, Chicago has over 200 theatres. Some of them form for one show, then disappear. Some have been around for a while. Most of them, though, are in the in-between stages, fueled by the passion of the actors and directors who are taking advantage of Chicago's theatrical climate to put forth their unique visions.

Following is a listing of Chicago-area theatre companies that have produced more than one show in the last year. We surveyed many different companies and most of the theatres responded. Those who didn't are listed with their address and phone numbers, so you can call them yourselves to find out what their policies are.

Chicago Area Theatre Companies

Chicago is unique in the vast number of theatres and theatre companies producing within and around its borders. Due to this bounty, a comprehensive list of these companies is virtually impossible. What follows is a list of Chicago theatre companies that have produced in the last few years. Information on their audition policies follows when available.

A Red Orchid Theatre
1531 N. Wells
Chicago, IL 60610
312/943-8722
312/943-9185 - fax
Equity - CAT N
Ensemble based
Generals - Fall
Open casting show by show
Keeps headshots on file

The Aardvark
1539 N. Bell
Chicago, IL 60622
773/489-0843
Open casting show by show
Keeps headshots on file

About Face Theatre
3212 N. Broadway
Chicago, IL 60657
773/549-7943

Alphabet Soup Productions
P.O. Box 85
Lombard, IL 60148
630/932-1555

American Eagle Productions
3914 N. Claremont
Chicago, IL 60618
773/539-1973

American Theatre Company
3855 N. Lincoln
Chicago, IL 60613
773/929-1031
Equity - CAT N
Ensemble based
Generals - Fall
Open casting show by show
Keeps headshots on file

Annoyance Theater
3747 N. Clark
Chicago, IL 60613
773/929-6200

Apple Tree Theatre
595 Elm Place
Highland Park, IL 60035
847/432-4335
847/432-5214 - fax
Equity
Generals - Unifieds
Keeps headshots on file

Azusa Productions
1639 W. Estes
Chicago, IL 60626
312/409-4207

Bailiwick Repertory
1229 W. Belmont
Chicago, IL 60657
773/883-1090
773/833-1091
Equity - CAT N
Open casting show by show
Keeps headshots on file

Barrington Area Arts Council Theatre in the Gallery
207 Park Avenue
P.O. Box 1266
Barrington, IL 60011-1266
847/382-5626
Open casting show by show
Keeps headshots on file

Beverly Theatre Guild
262 Cedarwood
Bolingbrook, IL 60440
773/238-0742
Generals - Fall
Open casting show by show
Keeps headshots on file

Black Ensemble Theatre
Artistic Director: Jackie Taylor
4520 N. Beacon
Chicago, IL 60640
773/769-5516
773/769-4451
773/769-5533 - fax
Equity
Some ensemble
Generals - Fall, January
Open casting show by show
Keeps headshots on file

Blue Rider Theatre
1822 S. Halsted
Chicago, IL 60608
312/733-4668

Bog Theatre
620 Lee Street
Des Plaines, IL 60016
847/296-0622
Equity - CAT N
Generals - August/September
Open casting show by show
Keeps headshots on file

Borealis Theatre Company
P.O. Box 2443
Aurora, IL 60507
630/844-4928
630/844-5515 - fax
Open casting show by show
Keeps headshots on file

Breadline Theatre Group
Paul Kampf, Artistic Director
6829 N. Lincoln Avenue #138
Lincolnwood, IL 60646
773/275-4342
Call to fax same number
Ensemble based
Keeps headshots on file
Our work is firmly entrenched in the belief in the actor as complete creative artist. All Breadline shows are developed through a collaboration of playwright, actor & director, resulting in a coming together of ideas from all members of the group. We are dedicated to the development of new works which incorporate a bold and inno-vative theatrical style. We cast show-to-show, but generally do not hold auditions. We invite artists interested and familiar with our work to contact us via mail, phone or email (BREADTHGRP@aol.com) We keep a file of all P/R submissions, but generally do not hold auditions.

Buffalo Theatre Ensemble
College of DuPage Arts Center
42 S. 22nd Street
Glen Ellyn, IL 60137
630/858-2800 x2100

Center Theatre Ensemble
1346 W. Devon
Chicago, IL 60660
773/508-0200
773/508-5422
773/508-9584 - fax
Equity - Tier N
Ensemble based
Generals - Summer/Unifieds
Open casting show by show
Keeps headshots on file

Centerlight Theatre
3444 Dundee Road
Northbrook, IL 60062
847/559-0110 x237
847/559-0110 x228
847/559-8199 - fax

Chicago Actors Studio Theater
1567 N. Milwaukee
Chicago, IL 60622
773/645-0222
773/645-0040 - fax
Some Ensemble.
Generals - Summer.
Open casting show by show

Chicago Children's Theatre
Scott Fergusson, Nan Zabriskie,
Artistic Directors
1806 W. Greenleaf
Chicago, IL 60626
773/262-9848
Generals - Fall
Open casting show by show
Keeps headshots on file

Chicago Dramatists Workshop
1105 W. Chicago
Chicago, IL 60622
312/633-0630
312/633-0610 - fax
Equity
Generals - Monthly
Open casting show by show
Keeps headshots on file

Chicago Opera Theatre
P.O. Box 39270
Chicago, IL 60639
773/292-7521
733/862-8094 - fax
Equity
Generals - Mid-Winter
Open casting show by show
Keeps headshots on file

Chicago Theatre Company
500 East 67th Street
Chicago, IL 60637
773/493-5502
Equity - CAT N
Open casting show by show
Keeps headshots on file

Chicago Theatreworks
773/868-9746

Child's Play Touring Company
2518 W. Armitage
Chicago, IL 60647
773/235-8911
773/235-5478 - fax
Ensemble based
Generals - Varies
Open casting show by show
Keeps headshots on file

Theatres

Children's Theatre Fantasy Orchard
P.O. Box 25084
Chicago, IL 60625
773/539-4211
Generals - Fall
Open casting show by show
Keeps headshots on file

Circle Theatre
7300 W. Madison Street
Forest Park, IL 60130
708/771-0700
Open casting show by show
Keeps headshots on file

City Lit
3212 N. Broadway
Chicago, IL 60657
773/784-8347
Generals - Unifieds
Keeps headshots on file

Classics On Stage, Ltd.
P.O. Box 25365
Chicago, IL 60625
773/989-0532
773/989-0598
Equity - TYA
Open casting show by show
Keeps headshots on file

Claudia Cassidy Series
312/742-1079
Equity - Staged Reading
Open casting show by show
Keeps headshots on file

Close Call Theatre
511 W. Belmont #47
Chicago, IL 60657
312/409-3274
Ensemble based

Open casting show by show
Keeps headshots on file

ComedySportz
3210 N. Halsted - 3rd floor
Chicago, IL 60657
773/549-8080
773/549-8142 - fax

Court Theatre
5535 S. Ellis Avenue
Chicago, IL 60637
773/702-7242
Equity - CAT V
Generals - Summer
Open casting show by show
Keeps headshots on file

Cranberry Productions
Shear Madness
636 S. Michigan
Chicago, IL 60605
312/786-9317
312/786-9177 - fax
Equity
Generals - Periodically
Open casting show by show
Keeps headshots on file

Curious Theatre Branch
2827 N. Lincoln
Chicago, IL 60657
773/327-6666

Defiant Theatre
4332 N. Hermitage #3W
Chicago, IL 60613
312/409-0585

Des Plaines Theatre Guild
3176 North Broadway #8
Chicago, IL 60657
312/425-8050
Open casting show by show

Dolphinback Theatre
1428 W. Winnemac #2W
Chicago, IL 60640
773/784-1789
Ensemble
Generals - Summer
Keeps headshots on file

The Drama Group
P.O. Box 594
Chicago Heights, IL 60411
708/754-5000
Open casting show by show

DreamStreet Theatre & Cabaret
12952 S. Western Avenue
Blue Island, IL 60406
708/371-5282
Equity - CAT II
Open casting show by show
Keeps headshots on file

**Drury Lane Theatre-
Evergreen Park**
2500 W. 95th Street
Evergreen Park, IL 60805
708/422-0404
708/422-8013 - fax
Equity
Generals (children's show) - January
Open casting show by show
Keeps headshots on file

Drury Lane Oakbrook
100 Drury Lane
Oakbrook Terrace, IL 60181
630/530-8300
630/530-0111
Equity - Dinner Theatre-L/TYA-PP

Emanon Theatre
3712 N. Broadway #356
Chicago, IL 60613
847/675-2200 x178

Equity Library Theatre Chicago
345 W. Dickens
Chicago, IL 60614
773/743-0266

ETA Creative Arts
7558 S. Chicago Avenue
Chicago, IL 60619
773/752-3955
Open casting show by show
Keeps headshots on file

European Repertory
Dale Goulding, Yasen Peyankov,
Artistic Directors
615 W. Wellington Avenue
UCC, Courtyard Entrance
Chicago, IL 60657
773/248-0577
773/248-0523 - fax
Ensemble based
Open casting show by show
Keeps headshots on file

Excaliber Shakespeare
4250 W. North Avenue
Chicago, IL 60639
Generals - Summer
Open casting show by show
Keeps headshots on file

Face to Face Productions
7329 W. Fitch
Chicago, IL 60631-1012
773/631-2013
Ensemble based
Keeps headshots on file

Factory Theatre
1257 N. Loyola Avenue
Chicago, IL 60626
773/274-1345
Ensemble based
Keeps headshots on file

Theatres

Famous Door Theatre
P.O. Box 57029
Chicago, IL 60657
773/404-8283
Equity
Ensemble based

First Folio Shakespeare Festival
146 Juliet Court
Clarendon Hills, IL 60514
630/986-8067
Equity

Fleetwood-Jourdain Theatre
2010 Dewey Avenue
Evanston, IL 60201
847/328-5740
Open casting show by show
Keeps headshots on file

Footsteps Theatre Company
5230 N. Clark Street
Chicago, IL 60640
773/878-4840
Ensemble based
Generals - Unifieds
Open casting show by show
Keeps headshots on file

Fourth Wall Productions
4300 N. Narragansett
Chicago, IL 60634
773/481-8535
773/481-8037 - fax
Generals - August
Open casting show by show
Keeps headshots on file

Free Associates
750 W. Wellington
Chicago, IL 60657
773/327-9917
Generals - August
Open casting show by show
Keeps headshots on file

Frump Tucker Theatre Company
P.O. Box 118315
Chicago, IL 60611
312/409-2689

Goodman Theatre
200 S. Columbus Drive
Chicago, IL 60603
312/443-4940
Equity - LORT
Generals - Summer
Open casting show by show

greasy joan & company
P.O. Box 267995
Chicago, IL 60626
773/761-8284
Equity

Griffin Theatre
5404 N. Clark
Chicago, IL 60640
312/784-8347
Open casting show by show
Keeps headshots on file

HealthWorks Theatre
3171 N. Halsted
Chicago, IL 60657-4435
773/929-4260
Ensemble based
Generals - July, December
Keeps headshots on file

hOstage tHeatre cO.
6934 N. Sheridan Road #3
Chicago, IL 60626
312/905-2212
Generals - May/June
Open casting show by show
Keeps headshots on file

Illinois Theatre Center
400A Lakewood Boulevard
Park Forest, IL 60466
708/481-3510
Equity - CAT III
Generals - July
Open casting show by show
Keeps headshots on file

Imagination Theatre
773/929-4100

ImprovOlympic
3541 N. Clark
Chicago, IL 60657
773/880-9993

Inclusive Theatre
640 N. LaSalle #535
Chicago, IL 60610
312/295-2754
Ensemble based
Generals - January/February
Open casting show by show
Keeps headshots on file

International Performance Studio
1517 W. Fullerton
Chicago, IL 60614
773/929-5437

Kaleidoscope Learning Theatre
P.O. Box 114
New Lenox, IL 60451
815/723-7928
815/723-7928 - fax

Kidworks Touring Theater Company
923 W. Gordon Terrace
Chicago, IL 60613
773/883-9932

Latino Chicago Theatre Company
1625 N. Damen
Chicago, IL 60647
773/486-5151
Equity
Generals - Fall
Open casting show by show
Keeps headshots on file

LeTraunik Productions, Inc.
430 Western Street
Hoffman Estates, IL 60194
847/885-8989
Open casting show by show

Lifeline Theatre
6912 N. Glenwood
Chicago, IL 60626
773/761-0667
Equity - CAT N
Open casting show by show
Keeps headshots on file

Live Bait Theatre
3914 N. Clark
Chicago, IL 60613
773/871-1212

Lookingglass Theatre Company
1229 W. Belmont
Chicago, IL 60657
847/864-7400
Equity
Ensemble based

Marquee Theatre Company
P.O. Box 6364
Evanston, IL 60204
847/604-0535
Open casting show by show
Keeps headshots on file

Marriott's Lincolnshire Theatre
10 Marriott Drive
Lincolnshire, IL 60069
847/634-0204
847/634-7358 - fax
Equity - Dinner Theatre 6/TYA-PP

Mary-Arrchie Theatre
731 W. Sheridan
Chicago, IL 60613
773/871-0442

The Moving Dock Theatre Company
2970 N. Sheridan Road #1021
Chicago, IL 60657
312/409-4714

The Mystery Shop
Mary Heitert
551 Sundance Court
Carol Stream, IL 60188
630/690-1105

National Pastime Theater
4139 N. Broadway
Chicago, IL 60613
773/327-7077
773/327-7422 - fax

Neo-Futurists
5153 N. Ashland
Chicago, IL 60640
773/275-5255
773/878-4557 - fax

New American Theatre
118 N. Main
Rockford, IL 61101
815/963-9454
815/963-7215 - fax
Equity - SPT
Generals - June
Open casting show by show
Keeps headshots on file

New Tuners Theatre
1225 W. Belmont
Chicago, IL 60657
773/929-7367 x10
Generals - Unifieds
Open casting show by show
Keeps headshots on file

Next Theatre
927 Noyes Street
Evanston, IL 60201
847/475-6763
Equity - CAT N
Generals - Summer
Open casting show by show
Keeps headshots on file

Northlight Theatre
9501 N. Skokie Boulevard
Skokie, IL 60076
312/633-1992
Equity - LORT
Open casting show by show
Keeps headshots on file

Oak Park Festival Theatre
P.O. Box 4114
Oak Park, IL 60303
708/524-2050
Equity
Generals - February/March
Open casting show by show
Keeps headshots on file

Onyx Theatre Ensemble
1020 W. Bryn Mawr
Chicago, IL 60660
773/561-5672
Equity - CAT N

Organic Touchstone Company
2851 N. Halsted
Chicago, IL 60657
773/477-5779
773/477-8993 - fax
Equity - CAT II
Generals - Unifieds/Equity in June
Open casting show by show
Keeps headshots on file

Pegasus Players
Truman College
1145 W. Wilson
Chicago, IL 60640
773/878-9761
Open casting show by show
Keeps headshots on file

Pendragon Players
4530 S. Avers Avenue
Chicago, IL 60632
773/890-1962

Perceptual Motion Inc. Dance Company
4057 N. Damen

Chicago, IL 60618
773/549-3958
773/883-1693 - fax

Pheasant Run Dinner Theatre
4051 E. Main
St. Charles, IL 60174
630/584-6300
Open casting show by show
Keeps headshots on file

Piven Theatre Workshop
927 Noyes #102
Evanston, IL 60201
847/866-6597
847/866-6614 - fax

Porchlight Theatre
1019 W. Webster
Chicago, IL 60614
773/325-9884

Powertap Productions
773/281-0022

Profiles Theatre
3761 N. Racine (mailing address)
Chicago, IL 60613
773/549-1815
312/944-4018 - fax
Ensemble based
Generals- August/September
Open casting show by show
Keeps headshots on file

Prologue Theatre Productions
1525 East 53rd Street #621
Chicago, IL 60615
773/248-7680
Open casting show by show
Keeps headshots on file

Prop Thtr
2621 N. Washtenaw - 1st floor
Chicago, IL 60647
773/486-7767
773/486-7767 - fax
Generals - Once a year
Open casting show by show
Keeps headshots on file

Raven Theatre
6931 N. Clark
Chicago, IL 60626
773/338-2177

Redmoon Theatre
2936 N. Southport - 1st floor
Chicago, IL 60657
773/388-9031
Keeps headshots on file

Rivendell Theatre Ensemble
1711 W. Belle Plaine #3
Chicago, IL 60613
773/472-1169
Equity - CAT N
Ensemble based
Open casting show by show
Keeps headshots on file

Roadworks Productions
1532 North Milwaukee Avenue
Chicago, IL 60622
773/489-ROAD
Equity - CAT N
Ensemble based
Open casting show by show
Keeps headshots on file

Saint Sebastian Players
1641 W. Diversey
Chicago, IL 60614
773/404-7922
Ensemble based

Open casting show by show
Keeps headshots on file

Second City
1616 N. Wells
Chicago, IL 60614
312/664-3959
312/664-9837 - fax
Equity - Special Agreement
Ensemble based
Keeps headshots on file

Shakespeare Repertory
820 N. Orleans #345
Chicago, IL 60610
312/642-8394
Equity - CAT V
Generals - Spring, Fall
Open casting show by show
Keeps headshots on file

Shattered Globe Theatre
2856 N. Halsted
Chicago, IL 60657
773/404-1237
Ensemble based
Open casting show by show
Keeps headshots on file

Shaw Chicago
312/742-1079
Equity - Staged Reading
Open casting show by show
Keeps headshots on file

Stage Left Theatre
3408 N. Sheffield
Chicago, IL 60657
773/883-8830
Ensemble based
Open casting show by show
Keeps headshots on file

Stage Right Dinner Theatre
236 E. Irving Park Road
Woodale, IL 60040
708/595-2044
Open casting show by show
Keeps headshots on file

Steppenwolf Theatre Company
1650 N. Halsted
Chicago, IL 60614
312/335-1888
Equity

Strawdog Theatre
3829 North Broadway
Chicago, IL 60613
773/528-9889
Equity - CAT N
Ensemble based
Generals - Unifieds
Open casting show by show
Keeps headshots on file

StreetSigns, Inc.
2202 N. Clark Street #213
Chicago, IL 60614
773/296-1875
Open casting show by show
Keeps headshots on file

Sweetback Productions
5013 N. Clark
Chicago, IL 60640
312/409-3925
Ensemble based
Open casting show by show
Keeps headshots on file

Teatro Vista
525 S. Cuyler
Oak Park, IL 60304
773/568-7871
Equity - CAT I
Ensemble based
Generals - Unifieds

Open casting show by show
Keeps headshots on file

Tempo Players
P.O. Box 386
Lombard, IL 60148
630/495-1120
Open casting show by show

Theatre at the Center
907 Ridge Road
Munster, IN 46321
219/836-3255
219/836-0130

Theatre Eclectic
630/548-2912
Ensemble based
Generals - September, January
Open casting show by show
Keeps headshots on file

Thirteenth Tribe
2012 W. Haddon
Chicago, IL 60622
773/252-2510
Open casting show by show

TinFish Productions
4223 N. Lincoln
Chicago, IL 60618
773/549-1888
Generals - August
Open casting show by show
Keeps headshots on file

Trap Door Theatre
1655 W. Cortland
Chicago, IL 60647
773/384-0494
773/384-2874
Ensemble based
Open casting show by show
Keeps headshots on file

Theatres

Tripaway Theatre
426 W. Surf #315
Chicago, IL 60657
773/868-0024
Ensemble based
Open casting show by show
Keeps headshots on file

Victory Gardens Theatre
2257 N. Lincoln
Chicago, IL 60614
773/549-5788
773/871-3000
773/549-2779 - fax
Equity - CAT IV
Generals - June
Open casting show by show
Keeps headshots on file

Waukegan Community Players
2641 Stewart Avenue
Evanston, IL 60201
Open casting show by show
Keeps headshots on file

Writer's Theatre Chicago
664 Vernon Avenue
Glencoe, IL 60022
847/835-5398
Equity - CAT II
Generals - Unifieds
Open casting show by show
Keeps headshots on file

XSIGHT! Performance Group
939 W. Ainslie #1E
Chicago, IL 60640
773/784-0992

Zeppo Productions
1815 W. Roscoe #1
Chicago, IL 60657
773/472-9902
Open casting show by show
Keeps headshots on file

The Joseph Jefferson Awards

Awards:

v.t. **1.** to give as merited or due: *to award prizes.* **2.** to assign by judicial decree. *n.* **3.** something awarded as a prize. **4.** the decision of an arbitrator.

If it be now; 'tis not to come; if it be not to come it will be now; if it be not now, yet it will come. The readiness is all.

By Carrie L. Kaufman

The Jeffs

The **Joseph Jefferson Awards,** or Jeffs as they're commonly called, started in 1967 when four actors got together to honor the best and brightest actors in Chicago. Six awards from seven theatres were given out at the first ceremony in 1968. Thirty years later, the Jeffs are split into three different sections, which gave out 86 awards from 244 nominations in 1997.

Equity Awards

The Equity wing of the Joseph Jefferson Awards judges theatres that have contracts with Actors Equity Association. **(For a discussion of actors' unions, see page 115.)**

Local Equity theatres are judged from August 1 to July 31, with an awards ceremony in November. They are formally called the Joseph Jefferson Awards. What an Equity actor, director, etc. wins that night is a Jeff Award. For years, the Equity Jeffs allowed only one winner per category. That all changed in 1997, when the Jeff Committee, under

Theatres

pressure from local area producers, opened up the Equity ballots to multiple winners. This was designed to enliven the ceremony, making it a celebration of good theatre rather than a competition. Whether it has worked or not is a matter of discussion.

What is clear is that the addition of lower tier Equity theatres has livened up the Jeff Awards. Now a CAT N theatre, which produced a show with only one Equity actor at a very low pay scale, can compete with a major LORT or CAT V theatre that has a budget in the millions and actually come out on top. This has done much to obliterate the distinctions between Equity and non-Equity theatre and also to showcase the remarkable work by people and theatre companies that are non-union — something which is unique to Chicago.

Non-Equity Citations

The **Citations wing** of the Joseph Jefferson Awards is for non-Equity theatres. The non-Equity wing was instituted in 1973. Citations are judged from April 1 to March 31, with a ceremony in early June. That ceremony is called the Joseph Jefferson Citations. The Jeff Committee is very careful to keep the word "award" as far away from non-Equity theatre as possible. That's because they structure the non-Equity ceremony to be completely non-competitive. There are "honorees," who may be called "winners," but there are absolutely no "losers." Of course, with the multiple recipients structure, there have been instances in which four out of the five people nominated have been "honored" with Citations, leaving a very clear "loser."

Touring Shows

About four years ago, the Jeff Committee began giving awards for touring productions, you know, *Les Miserables, Show Boat, Ragtime*. Frankly, these awards have little credibility in the theatre community and are often looked upon — rightly or wrongly — as opportunities for the Jeff Committee to get free tickets to the hot post-Broadway shows.

That may be a bit unfair. Jeff Committee members go to an awful lot of theatre and they deserve to see the big budget stuff. In addition, many local people get cast in touring shows. Why should the Jeff Committee ignore them? Frankly, if people are going to gripe about the Jeff Committee going to touring shows, they should gripe about critics going too. Neither make any difference to whether or not a show that size is a hit.

Eligibility

The Jeff Committee rules for eligibility are Byzantine. Barely anyone in Chicago theatre outside the Committee understands them, and I dare say there are some people on the Committee who would have trouble reciting every single rule. But if you work through the complexities, a remarkably fair and strangely beautiful system emerges.

There are two sets of rules. One qualifies theatres and shows to be judged. The other details exactly how a show is nominated or recommended — or not.

For a **show to be Jeff eligible** it must be produced at a theatre within a 30 mile radius of the corner of State and Madison. Some theatres — such as Marriott's Lincolnshire Theatre — were Jeff eligible before this rule was in place and have been grandfathered in.

For non-Equity theatres, the producing theatre must have been in existence for at least two years and produced at least four full-length shows during those two years, with at least two productions in the preceding year. Equity theatres are automatically eligible.

For an individual production to be Jeff eligible, it must have a minimum of 18 performances and run for a minimum of four weeks. In addition, it must have at least two consecutive weekend performances, with at least one weekend night performance per week available to Jeff members.

The Jeff Committee does not judge children's theatre, nor does it judge performance art. Late night shows — which are quite standard in Chicago — are also not eligible. Curtain for an eligible show must be no later than 9:30 p.m. This is not because the Jeff Committee does not like these things (many of them go to ineligible shows, just for fun); it's that they have to draw the line somewhere.

For judges to come to a theatre's opening night (or opening weekend) performance, the theatre must put in its request no later than three weeks before opening night. The Committee would rather have the requests five weeks prior. All requests must be in writing.

If the theatre is doing a co-production with another theatre, both theatres must be Jeff eligible. It doesn't matter how long the first theatre has been in existence — or how many Jeff Citations or Awards it has won in the past — if it hooks up with a brand new theatre company, the

Jeff Committee won't come.

These rules were instituted as a sort of filter. While there is much good theatre in Chicago, there is a lot of bad theatre here too and, frankly, the Jeff members don't want to waste their time. They figure that if a company has been able to attract audiences and stay afloat for two years, it must be doing some good stuff. Similarly, they feel that if a company is willing to take the risk of putting up an Equity bond and pay its actors, they know the company probably aren't fly-by-night.

Of course, this means that some really good theatre can't be nominated for a Jeff. Seanachai Theatre's *And Neither Have I Wings to Fly...* took Chicago audiences by storm in 1995, but wasn't Jeff eligible, even though many Jeff members saw the show on their own.

Nominating Process

Once the theatre has called the Jeff Committee and is deemed eligible, five Committee members are assigned to attend opening night of an Equity or non-Equity show. If those Jeff Committee members like the show or categories within the show — and it's non-Equity — then the show is **Recommended.** If the Jeff Committee members like the show — and it's Equity — then the show is **Nominated.**

Those recommendations and nominations come out the day after opening night. Judges must call in their votes by 11 a.m. and theatres are notified by 2 p.m. Essentially, in this phase the terms "recommended" and "nominated" mean the same thing, except one denotes that the show is non-Equity, the other that it's Equity.

What the terms "recommended" and "nominated" do not mean, however, is that the Jeff Committee is giving an unqualified endorsement of the show. A show that was particularly awful in all but one area could be recommended or nominated because the opening night judges thought that one area was so outstanding — maybe even because it was good despite the rest of the piece — that it deserves to be recognized.

How a show is deemed to be recommened or nominated is the most complicated part of the Jeff Committee's rules. There are two ways a show can get either recommended or nominated.

If three judges vote positively in any one category and a fourth judge votes positively in *any* category, then the show is recommended or nominated. For instance, if three judges loved and voted for the lead actress and a fourth judge loved and voted for the lead actor, even if the fifth judge hated the show entirely, the production is nominated. They don't have to like anything more about the show, though frequently if they like a show, they like it in multiple categories.

That last fact, and a few incidents in which judges have picked lots of categories but no three matched, prompted the Committee to add a second way shows can be recommended or nominated. If at least 10 positive votes — scattered across any of the categories — are cast by all five judges, and each one of the five casts at least one positive vote, then the production is recommended or nominated.

Once the show is either recommended or nominated, the rest of the Jeff Committee is informed and must see the show within 60 days of opening night. They are not told which categories the original five liked. They fax, e-mail or mail in their votes in each category after they've seen each show. Those votes are tabulated. The recipients of the most votes in each category are put onto a final ballot, which is sent out to each of the members at the end of the August 31 or March 31 judging season. Those final ballots are the *nominations* for each category — for both Equity and non-Equity theatres. It's confusing because the term "nomination" is used twice for Equity productions. I have no idea why.

After those Award and Citation nominations are made, the committee sends in those final ballots for the winners or recipients. The results of that vote are announced at either the November Awards or the June Citations.

Structure

The Jeff Committee is made up of 40 people dedicated to the theatre industry in Chicago. Quite simply, they love theatre. They see upwards of 125 shows a year and in the busy seasons — around September/October and February/March — they see around six shows a week. Many even see two shows a day on weekends when it's busy.

"This is a labor of love for people. You've got to love it if you're doing it for 125 nights a year with no compensation," says Joan Kaloustian, who is the current Jeff Committee chair.

As with any awards, there are people who don't like the Jeffs or who discount them. Funny though, Jeff Awards and Citations always seem to show up on people's resumes and in ads for shows or theatres. Some people have pointed to the Jeff Committee and said that there are few working theatre artists among its members. The Committee has countered with the fact that it has tried to recruit working theatre artists who balk at the idea of going to see someone else's show 4-6 nights a week.

The Jeff Committee members— no matter what their formal training — are always trying to learn more about theatre and the crafts that come together to make a show. Each meeting they have a speaker or program designed to help them learn more about stage crafts. Designers have taught them about the elements that are not supposed to be noticed. They have talked with directors and dramaturgs. And one cannot discount the point that no matter what one knows about theatre *before* joining the Committee, they learn a hell of a lot seeing 125 — often bad — shows. I wonder if many theatre artists have that kind of education.

Recently, the Jeff Committee has begun a dialogue with The League of Chicago Theatres on making some changes to the Jeffs. Sub-committees have been formed and ideas have been thrown out. Some have posited that the two ceremonies should be combined into one, in which both Equity Awards and non-Equity Citations would be given out.

See page 135 for a complete listing of The League.

Some have suggested that the Equity/non-Equity distinctions be obliterated altogether. Others have sought changes in the structure of the Committee; for instance, splitting the Committee up into 20 Equity and 20 non-Equity judges who would switch every year.

All of these suggestions are just that — suggestions, ideas. Kaloustian doesn't see any major changes happening this year, but she is grateful that the dialogue is happening. Theatre producers are beginning to understand that decisions are not quite as cut and dried as they thought. The Committee is understanding more what the producers want.

"The way we reached out to the theatres before was sort of informally," Kaloustian says. "Now that we have this forum for us to listen to the theatre community and for the community to hear our voice, [it] has made for a very strong team feeling, much stronger camaraderie than in the past few years."

To contact the Jeff Committee, call **773/388-0073.**

Living

F inally, actors have a host of other needs as they try to stay beautiful and trim, healthy and happy. Within this chapter lie the health clubs, skin care professionals, chiropractors and others who will keep you physically at your peak. Also, you'll find attorneys, movie theatres and more of the people and businesses that allow an actor to keep going in this wacky business.

Accountants and Tax Preparers

David Turrentine Income Tax Service
3907 N. Sacramento
Chicago, IL 60618
773/509-1798 • 773/509-1806 - fax

Jay-EMM Acct./Tax/Consulting
735 S. Victoria
Des Plaines, IL 60016
847/635-0136

Mangum, Smietanka & Johnson, LLC
35 E. Wacker Drive #2130
Chicago, IL 60601
312/368-8500 • 312/368-8534 - fax

H. Gregory Mermel
2835 N. Sheffield #311
Chicago, IL 60657
773/525-1778 • 312/525-3209 - fax

James P. Pepa, CPA
651 Hinman Ave. #3S
Evanston, IL 60202
847/491-1414 • 847/491-0740 - fax

Attorneys

Tom Fezzy
1163 E. Ogden Avenue
Naperville, IL 60565
630/548-3650
630/548-9764 - fax

JoAnne Guillemette
77 W. Wacker Drive #3200
Chicago, IL 60601
312/782-5437

Law Office of David P. Cudnowski, Ltd.
70 W. Madison #5330
Chicago, IL 60602
312/759-1040 • 312/759-1042 - fax

Law Offices of Joel N. Goldblatt, Ltd.
161 N. Clark Street #3575
Chicago, IL 60601-3293
312/372-9322 • 312/372-2905 - fax

Law Offices of William J. Borah
2024 Hickory Road
Homewood, IL 60430
708/799-0066
312/808-0066

Mangum, Smietanka & Johnson, LLC
35 E. Wacker Drive #2130

Chicago, IL 60601
312/368-8500
312/368-8534 - fax

Jay B. Ross & Associates
838 W. Grand #2W
Chicago, IL 60622-6565
312/633-9000
312/633-9090 - fax

Movies *The obscure and the inexpensive*

900 North Michigan Cinemas
900 N. Michigan
Chicago, IL 60611
312/787-1988

Biograph Theatre
2433 N. Lincoln Avenue
Chicago, IL 60614
773/348-4123

Cinema Chicago
1548 N. Clark
Chicago, IL 60622
312/951-6210

Esquire Theater
58 E. Oak
Chicago, IL 60611
312/280-0101

Facets Multimedia
1517 W. Fullerton
Chicago, IL 60614
773/281-9075

Lincoln Village Cinemas 1-6
6341 N. McCormick Road
Chicago, IL 60645
773/604-4747

Logan Theatre
2646 N. Milwaukee

Chicago, IL 60647
773/252-0627

McClurg Court Theatre
330 E. Ohio
Chicago, IL
312/642-0723

Music Box
3733 N. Southport
Chicago, IL 60613
773/871-6604

Three Penny Theatre
2424 N. Lincoln
Chicago, IL 60614
773/935-5744

The Vic Theatre (Brew & View)
3145 N. Sheffield
Chicago, IL 60657
773/472-0366 • 773/618-VIEW

Village North
6746 N. Sheridan
Chicago, IL 60626
773/764-9100

Village Theater
1548 N. Clark
Chicago, IL 60622
312/642-2403

Health & Fitness

Health Clubs

Bally Total Fitness
2828 N. Clark
Chicago, IL 60657
773/929-6900

Chicago Fitness Center
3131 N. Lincoln
Chicago, IL 60657
773/549-8181

Chicago Gym Jam
2727 N. Lincoln
Chicago, IL 60614
773/477-8400

Gold Coast Multiplex
1030 N. Clark Street
Chicago, IL 60610
312/944-1030

Know No Limits
3530 N. Lincoln
Chicago, IL 60657
773/404-1950

Lakeshore Athletic Clubs
441 N. Wabash
Chicago, IL 60611
312/644-4880

Lakeshore Athletic Clubs - Lincoln Park
1320 W. Fullerton
Chicago, IL 60614
773/477-9888

Lehmann Sports Club
2700 N. Lehmann Court
Chicago, IL 60614
773/871-8300

Riviera Health Club
400 E. Randolph - 7th floor
Chicago, IL 60601
312/527-2525

Webster Fitness Club
957 W. Webster Avenue
Chicago, IL 60614
773/248-2006
773/248-3195 - fax

Women's Workout World
1031 N. Clark
Chicago, IL 60610
312/664-2106

World Gym
100 S. Wacker
Chicago, IL 60606
312/357-WRLD

Health Food Stores

Great Earth
2810 N. Clark Street
Chicago, IL 60657
773/281-1211

Life Spring
3178 N. Clark
Chicago, IL 60657
773/327-1023

Sherwyn's
645 W. Diversey
Chicago, IL 60614
773/477-1934 • 773/477-6632 - fax

Whole Foods Market
1000 W. North Avenue
Chicago, IL 60622
312/587-0648

Nutritionists

Lifelink Medical Center
Dr. Craig H. Jacobus
64 Orland Square Drive #101
Orland Park, IL 60462
708/361-9552

Rose Quest Nutrition Center
200 N. Michigan #404A
Chicago, IL 60602
312/444-9234

Weight Control

Weight Watchers
800/651-6000

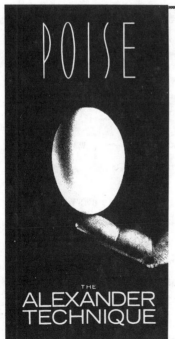
Living

Counselors

**Abraham Lincoln Center
Screening & Support**
1950 W. 87th
Chicago, IL 60620
773/239-7960

Community Counseling Center
5710 N. Broadway
Chicago, IL 60660
773/728-1000
773/728-6517 - fax

**Community Counseling Center
of Chicago**
Mental Health Center
4740 N. Clark
Chicago, IL 60640
773/769-0205
773/769-0344 - fax

Panic Anxiety Recovery Center
680 N. Lake Shore Drive
Chicago, IL 60611
312/642-7954

**Jason Simpson and Michael
Sheahan**
888/415-1530

Dr. Steigman
4433 W. Touhy
Lincolnwood, IL 60646
847/675-7544

Hypnotists

**Associated Psychologists
and Therapists**
625 N. Michigan Avenue #1225
Chicago, IL 60611
312/630-1001

Dr. Steigman
4433 W. Touhy
Lincolnwood, IL 60646
847/675-7544

Sun Center
1816 N. Wells St.
Chicago, IL 60614
312/280-1070

Chiropractors

**Chicago Neck and Back
Institute**
5720 W. Fullerton #1
Chicago, IL 60639
773/237-8660
773/237-3159 - fax

Chislof Chiropractic Center
7448 N. Harlem
Chicago, IL 60631
773/763-0400

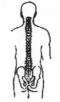
Living

Graham Chiropractic
Dr. Betty E. Graham
5344 N. Lincoln
Chicago, IL 60625
773/769-6666
773/334-1696 - fax

Greater Chicago Chiropractic
Dr. Dale Zuehlke
561 W. Diversey Parkway #221
Chicago, IL 60614
773/871-7766

Lifelink Medical Center
Dr. Craig H. Jacobus
64 Orland Square Drive #101
Orland Park, IL 60462
708/361-9552

Lakeshore Chiropractic Health Center
Dr. Ellisa J. Grossman
3125 N. Halsted
Chicago, IL 60657
773/935-9595
773/935-5869 - fax

Progressive Chiropractic
Rehabilitation & Wellness Center
2816 N. Sheffield
Chicago, IL 60657
773/525-WELL
773/525-9397 - fax

Dr. Kevin Regan
55 E. Washington #1641
Chicago, IL 60602
312/578-1624
312/346-6530 - fax

Stiles Chiropractic Services
1 E. Superior #201
Chicago, IL 60611
312/642-1138
312/642-1349 - fax

Wellness Group
707 Lake Cook Road #303
Deerfield, IL 60015
847/559-9355
847/559-9359 - fax

Naprapaths

Belmont Health Care
2110 W. Belmont
Chicago, IL 60618
773/404-0909

Chicago National College of Naprapathy
3330 N. Milwaukee
Chicago, IL 60641
773/282-2686

Lake Shore Naprapathic Center
3166 N. Lincoln Avenue #410
Chicago, IL 60657
773/327-0844

Naprapathic Clinic
1520 E. Roosevelt
Wheaton, IL 60187-6806
630/871-3031

Acupuncture

Chicago Acupuncture Clinic
3723 N. Southport
Chicago, IL 60613
773/871-0342

Graham Chiropractic
Dr. Betty E. Graham
5344 N. Lincoln
Chicago, IL 60625
773/769-6666
773/334-1696 - fax

Illinois State Acupuncture Association
Chicago, IL
312/853-3765

Franklin D. Ing
2451 N. Lincoln
Chicago, IL 60614
773/525-2444

Know No Limits
3530 N. Lincoln
Chicago, IL 60657
773/404-1950

Lakeshore Chiropractic Health Center
Dr. Ellisa J. Grossman
3125 N. Halsted
Chicago, IL 60657
773/935-9595
773/935-5869 - fax

Progressive Chiropractic
Rehabilitation & Wellness Center
2816 N. Sheffield
Chicago, IL 60657
773/525-WELL
773/525-9397 - fax

Massage

American Massage Therapy Association
Illinois Chapter
708/354-2682

Bob Barret
Riviera Health Club
400 E. Randolph - 7th floor
Chicago, IL 60601
312/527-2525

Bodyscapes, Inc.
Massage Therapy Clinic
820 Davis #216
Evanston, IL 60201
847/864-6464

Sue Brown
2024 N. Holly
Chicago, IL 60614
773/862-9089

Chislof Chiropractic Center
7448 N. Harlem
Chicago, IL 60631
773/763-0400

Grand Experience
110 E. Delaware
Chicago, IL 60611
312/787-7876
312/787-8940 - fax

Living

Know No Limits
3530 N. Lincoln
Chicago, IL 60657
773/404-1950

Linda Fields Salon
919 N. Michigan #1923
Chicago, IL 60611
312/951-1188
312/951-1189 - fax

Massage Therapy Professionals
3047 N. Lincoln #400
Chicago, IL 60657
773/472-9484

Peace School
3121 N. Lincoln
Chicago, IL 60657
773/248-7959 • 773/248-7963 - fax

Rodica European Skin & Body Care Center
Water Tower Place - Professional Side
845 N. Michigan Avenue #944E
Chicago, IL 60611
312/527-1459

Sun Center
1816 N. Wells St.
Chicago, IL 60614
312/280-1070

Wellness Group
707 Lake Cook Road #303
Deerfield, IL 60015
847/559-9355
847/559-9359

Yoga

Global Yoga and Wellness Center
1608 N. Milwaukee #212
Chicago, IL 60647
773/489-1510

NU Yoga Center
3047 N. Lincoln – 3rd floor
Chicago, IL 60657
773/327-3650

Sivananda Yoga Center
1246 W. Bryn Mawr
Chicago, IL 60660
773/878-7771

Yoga Circle
401 W. Ontario
Chicago, IL
312/915-0750

Tai Chi

Tai Chi Chuan
John Kozak
708/447-0112

Dance Center of Columbia College
4730 N. Sheridan Road
Chicago, IL 60640
773/989-3310
773/271-7046- fax

AIDS Resources

Horizons Community Service
Gay and Lesbian Hotline
Chicago, IL
773/929-4357

ILL AIDS Hotline
800/590-2437

Spanish AIDS Hotline
(8am-2am)
800/344-7432

Stop AIDS
3651 N. Halsted
Chicago, IL 60613
773/871-3300
773/871-2528 - fax

Test Positive Aware Network
1258 W. Belmont
Chicago, IL 60657
773/404-8726

TTY AIDS Hotline
(10am-10pm) (24 hr. machine)
800/243-7889

Grooming & Appearance

Salons

Alfaro Hair Design
3454 N. Southport
Chicago, IL 60657
773/935-0202

Alpha Wave Hair Design Studio
2652 N. Halsted
Chicago, IL 60657
773/327-2200

The Beauty Salon
3732 N. Broadway
Chicago, IL 60613
773/327-8870

Curl Up and Dye
2837 N. Clark
Chicago, IL 60657
773/348-1000

Living

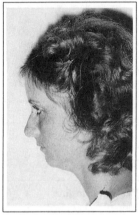

David's
3128 N. Lincoln Avenue
Chicago, IL 60657
773/472-2226

Diamond Beauty Clinic
151 N. Michigan Avenue #1018
Chicago, IL 60601
312/240-1042

Grand Experience
110 E. Delaware
Chicago, IL 60611
312/787-7876
312/787-8940 - fax

Hair Artists
Paul Rehder Salon
939 N. Rush
Chicago, IL 60611
312/943-7404

Hair Loft
14 E. Pearson
Chicago, IL 60611
312/943-5435

J. Gordon Designs, Ltd.
2326 N. Clark
Chicago, IL 60614
773/871-0770

Joseph Michaels Salon
715 N. State Street
Chicago, IL 60610
312/482-9800
312/482-9633 - fax

Linda Fields Salon
919 N. Michigan #1923
Chicago, IL 60611
312/951-1188
312/951-1189 - fax

Marianne Strokirk Salon
361 W. Chestnut
Chicago, IL 60610
312/944-4428
312/944-4429 - fax

**Mario Tricoci Hair Salon
& Day Spa**
277 E. Ontario
Chicago, IL 60611
312/915-0960

Molina Molina
19 E. Chestnut - 2nd floor
Chicago, IL 60611
312/664-2386

Niko
3200 N. Lake Shore Drive
Chicago, IL 60657
773/472-0883

Philip James
710 W. Diversey
Chicago, IL 60614
773/248-9880

Salon Absolu
1216 W. Belmont
Chicago, IL 60657
773/525-2396

Southport Hair Studio
3430 N. Southport Avenue
Chicago, IL 60657
773/477-9319

Timothy Paul Salon
200 E. Delaware
Chicago, IL 60611
312/944-5454

Trio
11 E. Walton
Chicago, IL 60611
312/944-6999

Living

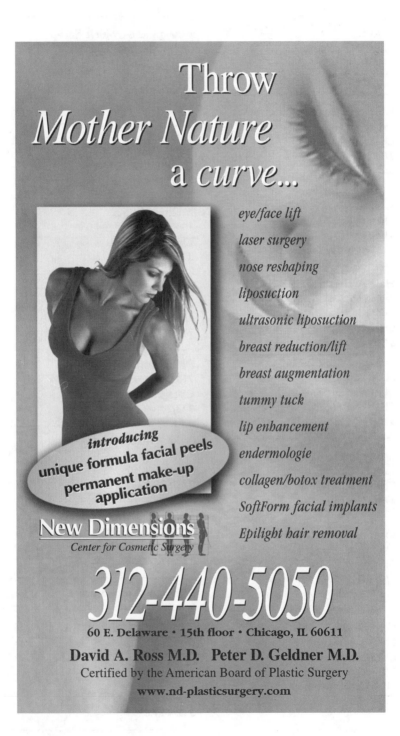

Cosmetic Surgery

Associated Plastic Surgeons
Dr. Robert Swartz
845 N. Michigan #934E
Chicago, IL 60611
312/787-5313
800/232-0767

Chicago Hair Institute
(Hair restoration/implants)
Ron Corniels
710 N. York Road
Hinsdale, IL 60521
708/655-9331

Dr. Diane L. Gerber
680 N. Lake Shore Drive #930
Chicago, IL 60611
312/654-8700

Dr. Myles E. Goldflies
455 E. Illinois #463
Chicago, IL 60611
312/943-8886 • 312/245-9969

Wafik A. Hanna, M.D.
12 Salt Creek Lane #225
Hinsdale, IL 60521
630/887-8180

Liposuction Institute of America
Dr. Leon Tcheupdjian
1700 W. Central Road
Arlington Heights, IL 60005
847/259-0100

New Dimensions Center for Cosmetic Surgery
60 E. Delaware – 15th floor
Chicago, IL 60611
312/440-5050
312/440-5064 - fax

Oakbrook Aesthetic
1 S. 224 Summit #310
Oakbrook Terrace, IL 60181
630/932-9690
630/932-8125 - fax

Skin Care

2 Salon
Nina Catalano
1017 W. Washington
Chicago, IL 60607
312/997-2233

Barbara's Skin Care
645 N. Michigan #420
Chicago, IL 60611
312/943-4728

European Skin Care
6305 N. Milwaukee
Chicago, IL 60646
773/763-6044

Femline Hair Designs, Inc.
3500 Midwest Road
Oakbrook, IL 60522
630/655-2212

Hair Loft
14 E. Pearson
Chicago, IL 60611
312/943-5435

Joseph Michaels Salon
715 N. State Street
Chicago, IL 60610
312/482-9800
312/482-9633 - fax

Living

**Mario Tricoci Hair Salon
& Day Spa**
277 E. Ontario
Chicago, IL 60611
312/915-0960

**Rodica European Skin & Body
Care Center**
Water Tower Place - Professional Side
845 N. Michigan Avenue #944E
Chicago, IL 60611
312/527-1459

Syd Simons Cosmetics, Inc.
2 E. Oak - 38th floor
Chicago, IL 60611
312/943-2333

Electrolysis

2 Salon
Nina Catalano
1017 W. Washington
Chicago, IL 60607
312/997-2233

Amber Electrolysis
3734 N. Southport
Chicago, IL 60613
773/549-3800

**Block Ltd. Permanent Hair
Removal**
166 E. Superior #502
Chicago, IL 60611
312/266-1350

Water Tower Hair Removal
845 N. Michigan #972 West
Chicago, IL 60611
312/787-4028

Dentists

**A Ashland Lincoln Family
Dental Center**
3120 N. Ashland Avenue
Chicago, IL 60657
773/281-7550

Belmont Dental Care
3344 N. Lincoln Avenue
Chicago, IL 60657
773/549-7971

Feldman, Feldman & Green
3423 N. Broadway
Chicago, IL 60657
773/477-8585

**Lincoln Park Columbus Dental
Associates**
2551 N. Clark #700
Chicago, IL 60614
773/348-7008

Lincoln Park Cosmetic and General Dentistry
424 W. Fullerton
Chicago, IL 60614
773/404-0101

Dr. Craig Millard, DDS, PC
30 N. Michigan
Chicago, IL 60602
312/726-5830

Michelle Rappeport, DDS
3208 N. Southport
Chicago, IL 60657
773/935-4960

Ravenswood Dental Group
1945 W. Wilson
Chicago, IL 60640
773/334-2227

Dr. Ieva Wright
333 N. Michigan #2900
Chicago, IL 60601
312/236-3226
312/236-9629 - fax

Wrigleyville Dental Group
1353 W. Cornelia
Chicago, IL 60657
773/975-6666

Public Service Phone Numbers

Attorney General
312/814-3000

CTA/PACE Information
312/836-7000

Equal Employment Opportunity
312/353-2713

IRS Taxpayer Information
800/829-1040

Chicago Park District
312/747-2200

Police (non emergency)
312/746-6000

Post Office Information
312/654-3895

Ticket Master
312/559-1950

Living

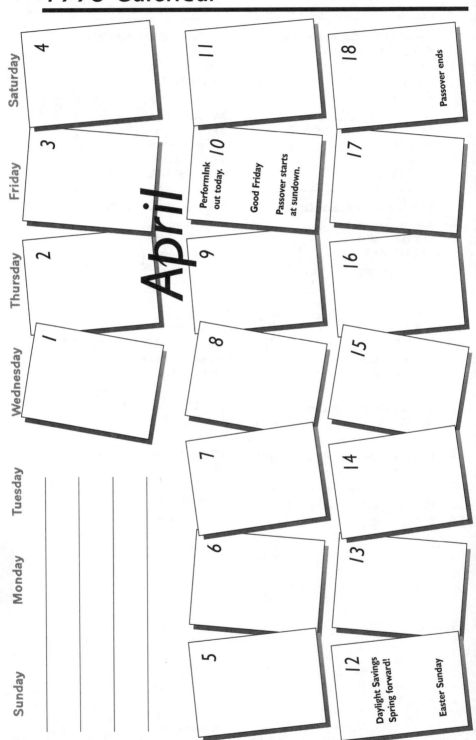

April

Sunday	Monday	Tuesday	Wednesday	Thursday	Friday	Saturday
			1	2	3	4
5	6	7	8	9	10 PerformInk out today. Good Friday Passover starts at sundown.	11
12 Daylight Savings Spring forward! Easter Sunday	13	14	15	16	17	18 Passover ends

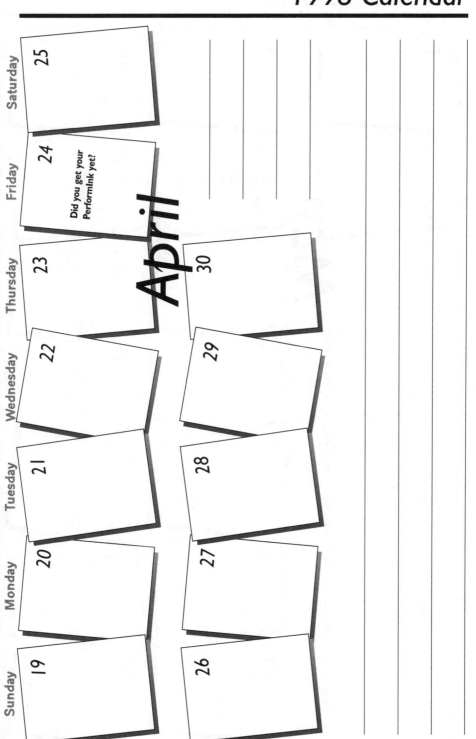

April

Sunday	Monday	Tuesday	Wednesday	Thursday	Friday	Saturday
19	20	21	22	23	24	25
26	27	28	29	30		

Did you get your PerformInk yet?

1998 Calendar

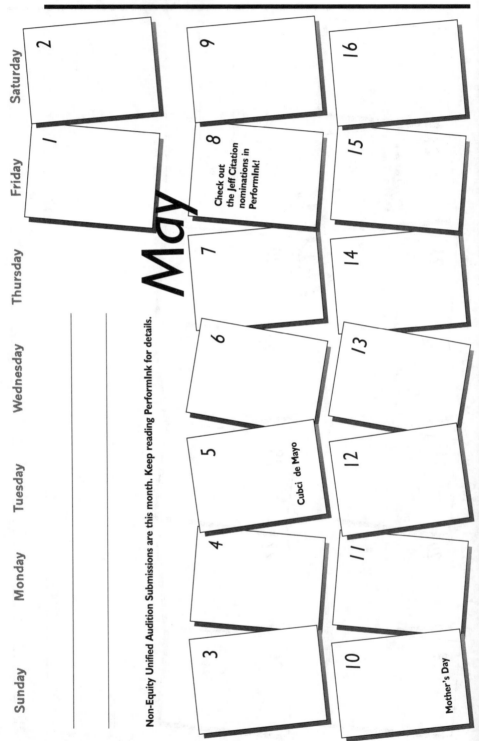

May

Sunday	Monday	Tuesday	Wednesday	Thursday	Friday	Saturday
					1	2
3	4	5	6	7	8 Check out the Jeff Citation nominations in PerformInk!	9
10 Mother's Day	11	12	13	14	15	16

Cubci de Mayo

Non-Equity Unified Audition Submissions are this month. Keep reading PerformInk for details.

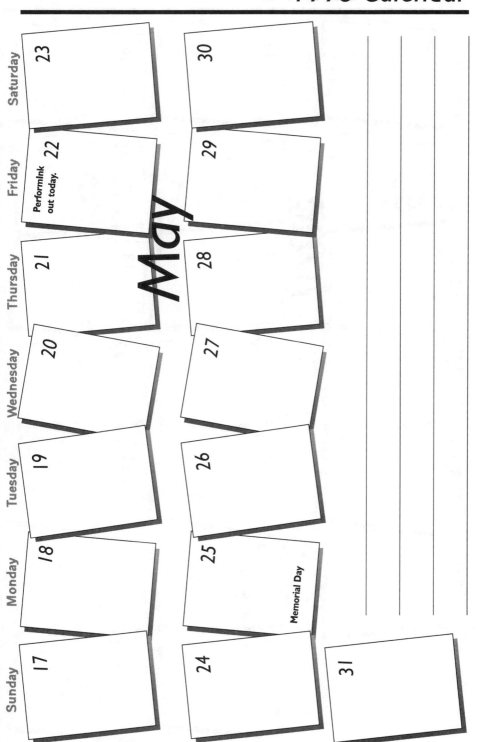

May

Sunday	Monday	Tuesday	Wednesday	Thursday	Friday	Saturday
17	18	19	20	21	22 PerformInk out today.	23
24	25 Memorial Day	26	27	28	29	30
31						

1998 Calendar

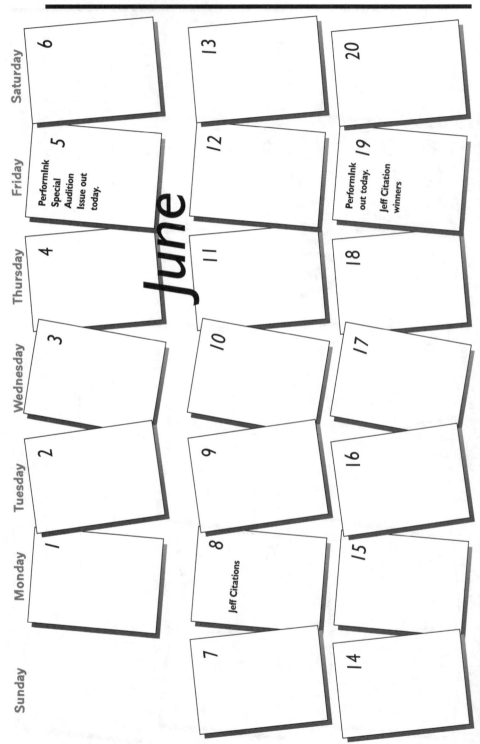

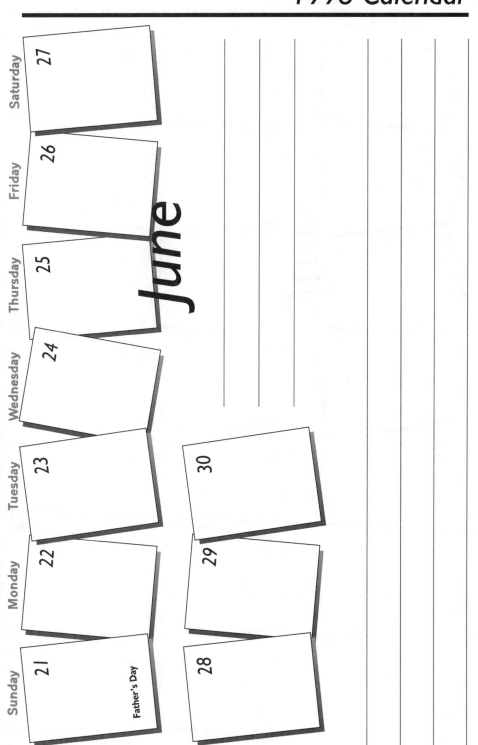

June

Sunday	Monday	Tuesday	Wednesday	Thursday	Friday	Saturday
21 Father's Day	22	23	24	25	26	27
28	29	30				

1998 Calendar

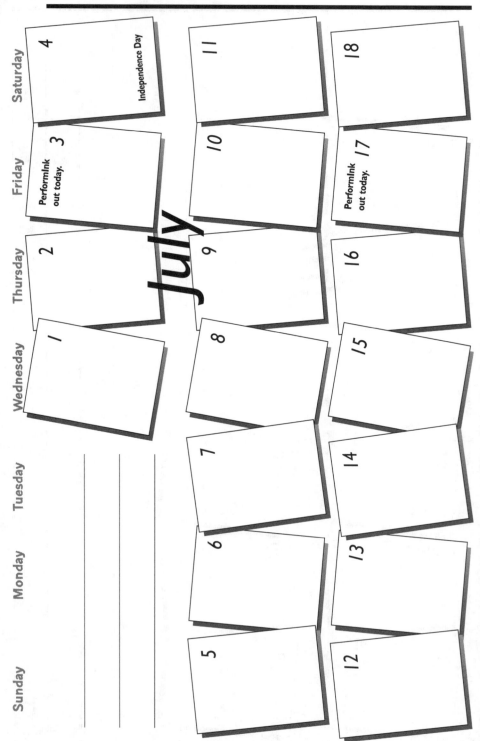

July

Sunday	Monday	Tuesday	Wednesday	Thursday	Friday	Saturday
			1	2	3 PerformInk out today.	4 Independence Day
5	6	7	8	9	10	11
12	13	14	15	16	17 PerformInk out today.	18

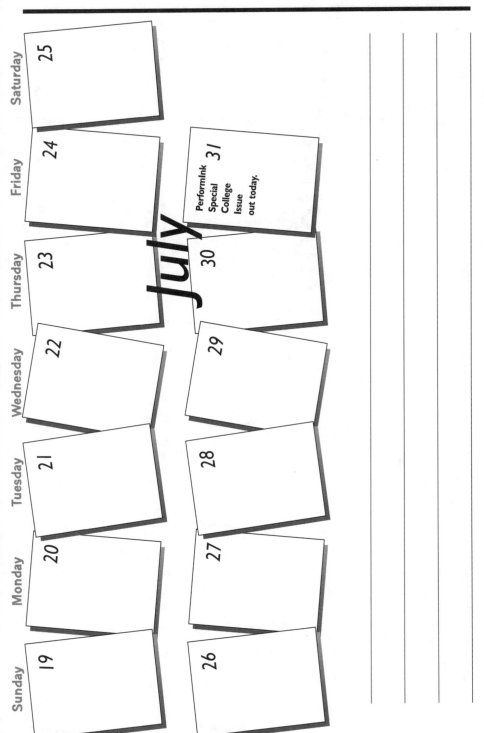

July

Sunday	Monday	Tuesday	Wednesday	Thursday	Friday	Saturday
19	20	21	22	23	24	25
26	27	28	29	30	31 PerformInk Special College Issue out today.	

1998 Calendar

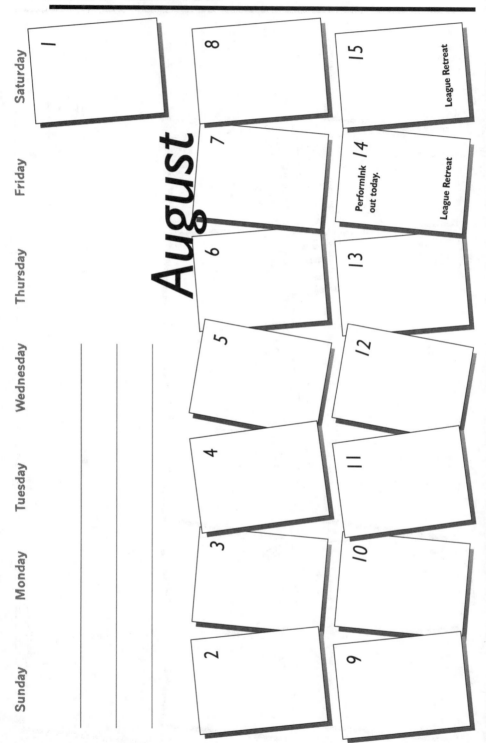

August

Sunday	Monday	Tuesday	Wednesday	Thursday	Friday	Saturday
						1
2	3	4	5	6	7	8
9	10	11	12	13	PerformInk 14 out today.	15
					League Retreat	League Retreat

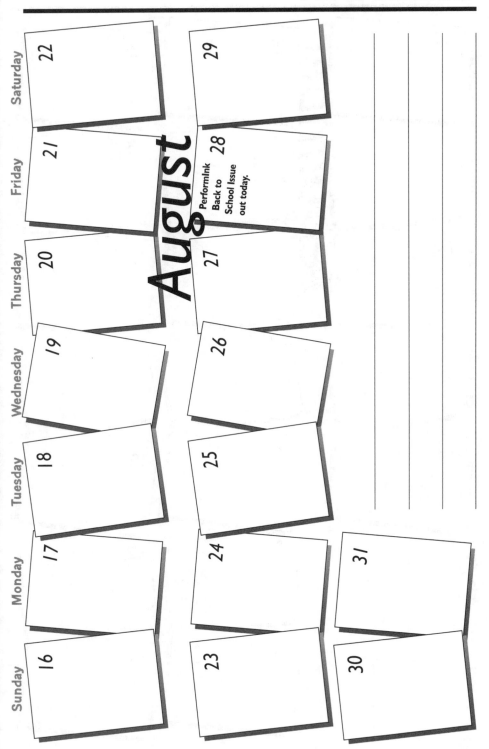

August

Sunday	Monday	Tuesday	Wednesday	Thursday	Friday	Saturday
16	17	18	19	20	21	22
23	24	25	26	27	28 **PerformInk Back to School Issue out today.**	29
30	31					

1998 Calendar

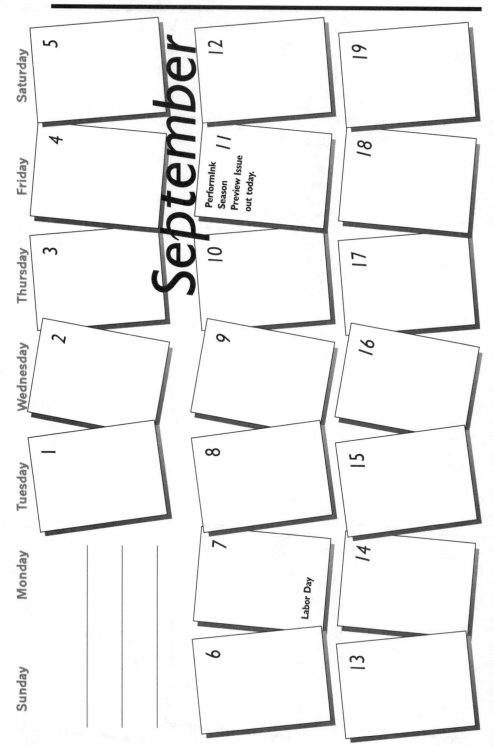

September

Sunday	Monday	Tuesday	Wednesday	Thursday	Friday	Saturday
		1	2	3	4	5
6	7 Labor Day	8	9	10	11 PerformInk Season Preview Issue out today.	12
13	14	15	16	17	18	19

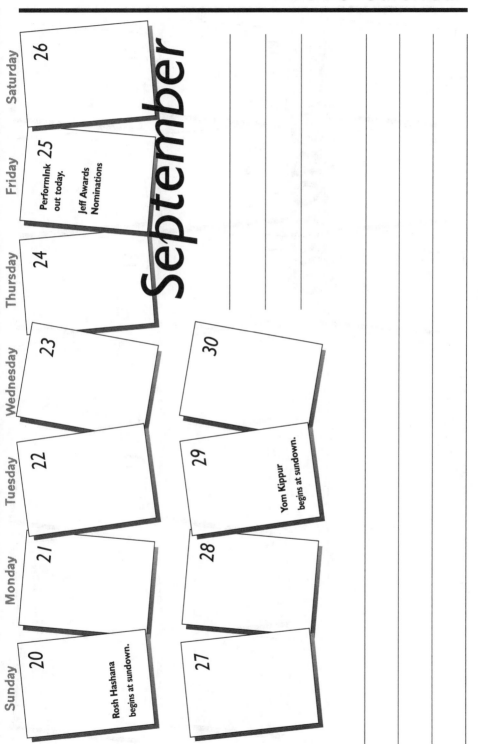

September

Sunday	Monday	Tuesday	Wednesday	Thursday	Friday	Saturday
20 **Rosh Hashana begins at sundown.**	21	22	23	24	25 **Performlnk out today.** **Jeff Awards Nominations**	26
27	28	29 **Yom Kippur begins at sundown.**	30			

1998 Calendar

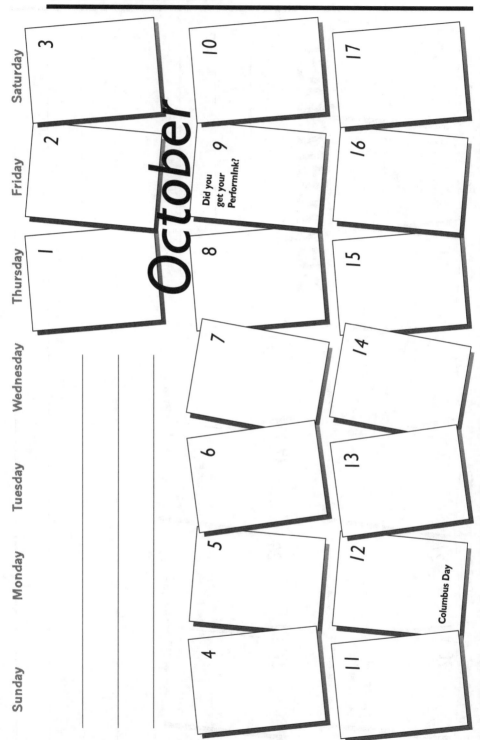

October

Sunday	Monday	Tuesday	Wednesday	Thursday	Friday	Saturday
				1	2	3
4	5	6	7	8	9 Did you get your PerformInk?	10
11	12 Columbus Day	13	14	15	16	17

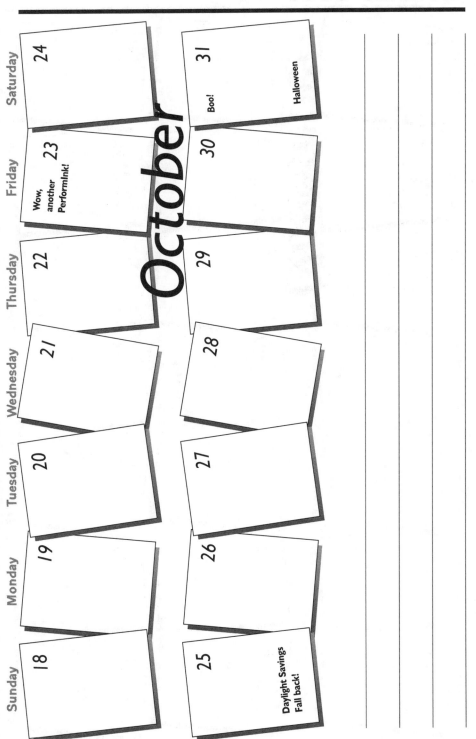

October

Sunday	Monday	Tuesday	Wednesday	Thursday	Friday	Saturday
18	19	20	21	22	23 Wow, another PerformInk!	24
25 Daylight Savings Fall back!	26	27	28	29	30	31 Boo! Halloween

1998 Calendar

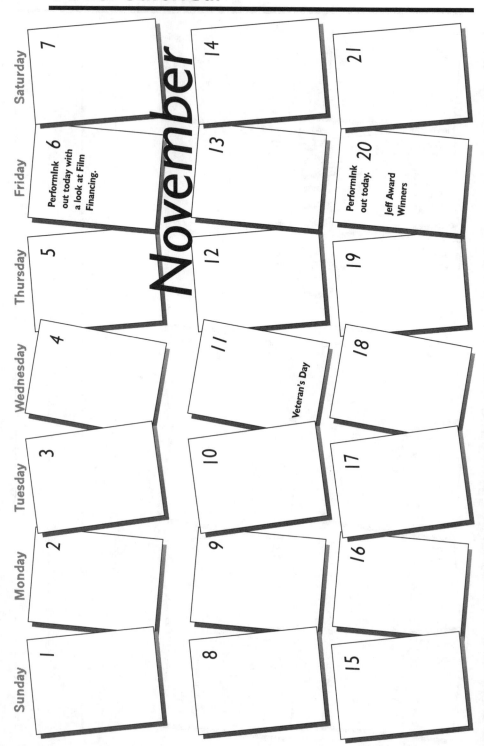

November

Sunday	Monday	Tuesday	Wednesday	Thursday	Friday	Saturday
1	2	3	4	5	6 **PerformInk out today with a look at Film Financing.**	7
8	9	10	11 Veteran's Day	12	13	14
15	16	17	18	19	20 **PerformInk out today.** Jeff Award Winners	21

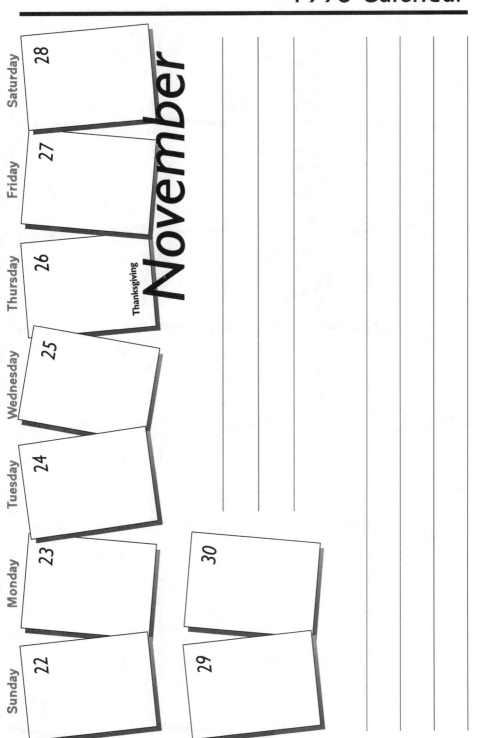

November

Sunday	Monday	Tuesday	Wednesday	Thursday	Friday	Saturday
22	23	24	25	26 Thanksgiving	27	28
29	30					

1998 Calendar

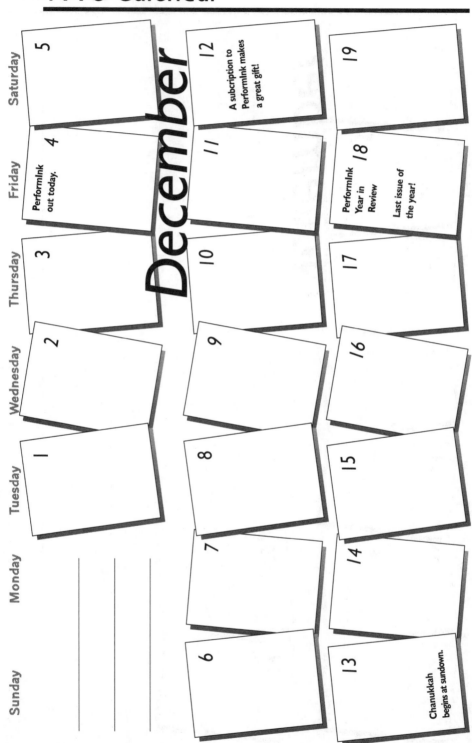

December

Sunday	Monday	Tuesday	Wednesday	Thursday	Friday	Saturday
		1	2	3	4 — PerformInk out today.	5
6	7	8	9	10	11	12 — A subcription to PerformInk makes a great gift!
13 — Chanukkah begins at sundown.	14	15	16	17	18 — PerformInk Year in Review. Last issue of the year!	19

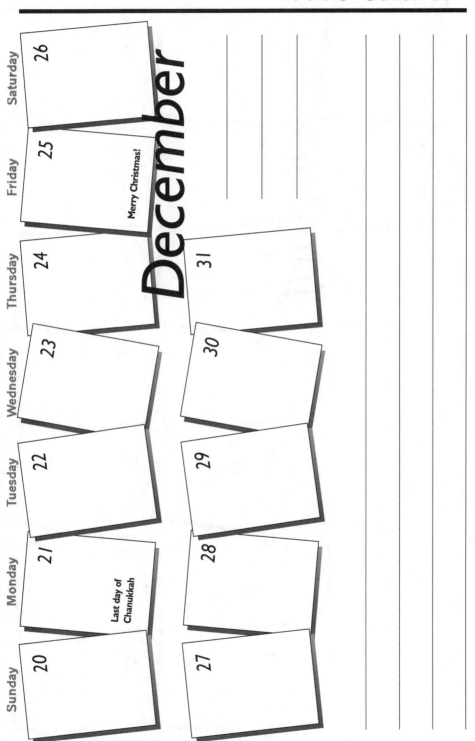

December

Sunday	Monday	Tuesday	Wednesday	Thursday	Friday	Saturday
20	21 Last day of Chanukkah	22	23	24	25 Merry Christmas!	26
27	28	29	30	31		

1999 Calendar

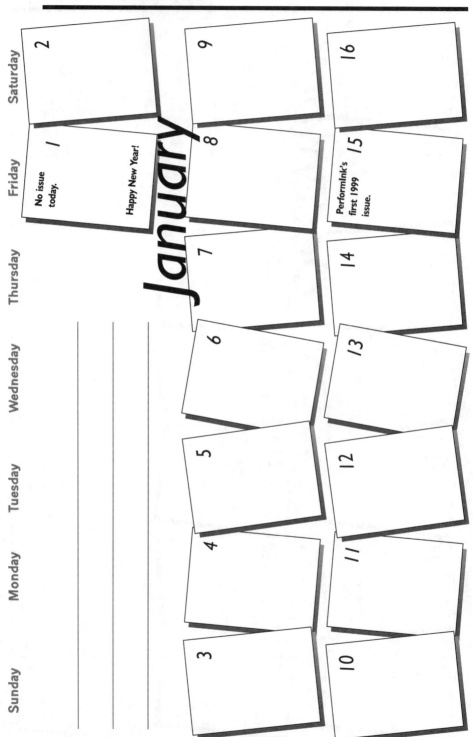

January

Sunday	Monday	Tuesday	Wednesday	Thursday	Friday	Saturday
					1 — No issue today.	2 — Happy New Year!
3	4	5	6	7	8	9
10	11	12	13	14	15 — PerformInk's first 1999 issue.	16

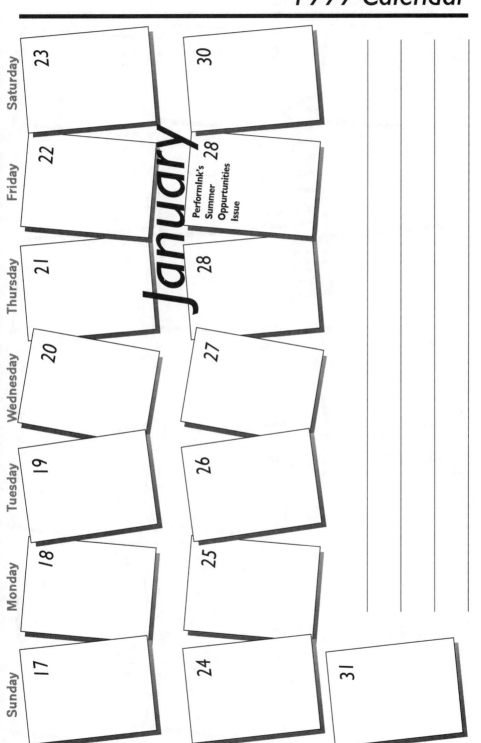

Sunday	Monday	Tuesday	Wednesday	Thursday	Friday	Saturday
17	18	19	20	21	22	23
24	25	26	27	28	28 PerformInk's Summer Oppurtunities Issue	30
31						

January

1999 Calendar

February

Saturday
6
13
20

Friday
5
12
PerformInk's Sundance coverage.
19

Thursday
4
11
18

Wednesday
3
10
17

Tuesday
2
9
16

Monday
1
8
15

Sunday
7
14

February

Sunday	Monday	Tuesday	Wednesday	Thursday	Friday	Saturday
21	22	23	24	25	15	27
28						

15 PerformInk preview. March film events.

1999 Calendar

March

Sunday	Monday	Tuesday	Wednesday	Thursday	Friday	Saturday
	1	2	3	4	5	6
7	8	9	10	11	12 PerformInk out today.	13
14 New edition of The Book: An Actor's Guide to Chicago on sale now.	15	16	17	18	29	20

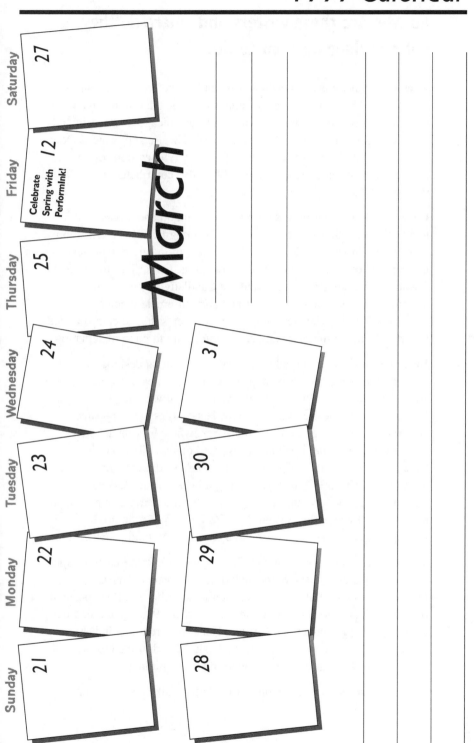

March

Sunday	Monday	Tuesday	Wednesday	Thursday	Friday	Saturday
21	22	23	24	25	12 **Celebrate Spring with PerformInk!**	27
28	29	30	31			

So who are these writers and where do they get off telling us what to do?

Adrianne Duncan is a Chicago actress and former vice president of The Actor's Connection. She has numerous film, television and commercial credits and has worked with multiple Chicago theatres, including Shakespeare Repertory, National Jewish Theatre and Famous Door. She collaborated extensively on the 1995 and 1996 editions of the acting guide, "Chicago Connection," and has also contributed to PerformInk Newspaper.

Christine Gatto is an actress currently working in and around her native Chicago. Since receiving a BFA in acting from Northern Illinois University, Chris has appeared with a variety of theatre companies including Close Call, Fourth Wall Productions, Circle Theatre, Borealis Theatre, Powertap Productions and the Candlelight Forum Theatre. In addition, Chris is a board member and core ensemble member of Kidworks Touring Theatre Company, a children's theatre company dedicated to bringing literature and education to life through imagination.

Kevin Heckman has worked as an actor and lighting designer in Chicago for over three years, appearing at Shakespeare Repertory, Apple Tree Theatre, Illinois Theatre Center, Bailiwick Repertory, Stage Left and Circle Theatre to name a few. His designs have appeared at Famous Door, Stage Left and Bailiwick, where he won an After Dark Award for *Rope*. In all he has worked on over 50 shows in Chicago. Additionally, he served on the board of directors of Symposium Theatre Company. Kevin graduated from Wesleyan University in Connecticut with degrees in theatre and mathematics, and has lived and worked in Boston, New York and San Antonio. In Chicago he is excited to have found a city that can hold his attention.

Tina O'Brien is the kids agent at Cunningham • Escott • DiPene. She has been an agent for six years, including five years at Harrise Davidson and Associates. Tina was a child actor herself. She appeared in numerous shows and productions in the early 1980's, including the Chicago touring production of Annie. Her exposure to the industry at a young age gave her an affinity for the business end of the business. She is a kids agent because she loves working with children.

Carrie L. Kaufman is the publisher of PerformInk Newspaper and PerformInk Books.

Advertiser's Index

Notes:

The

Book

An Actor's Guide
to Chicago

Notes:

The

ook

An Actor's Guide
to Chicago

Order a subscription to

Chicago's Entertainment Trade Paper. The art, the business, the industry.

Your source for vital industry news

PerformInk Newspaper is a biweekly (every 2 weeks) publication with news and information on the theatre and film industries in Chicago and the Midwest, including job listings and audition notices. Production listings are coming soon. PerformInk's mission is to be a catalyst in the healthy growth of the local film and theatre industries.

Name _____

Business Name_____

Address _____

City _____St _____Zip_____

Phone _____

Fax _____

e-mail _____

website_____

___Send me a 1-year subscriptions to PerformInk. I have enclosed my check or money order for $27.95. Please bill the credit card number below for $27.95.

___Send me a copy of the 1998 edition of "The Book: An Actor's Guide to Chicago" for $15 plus a $3 shipping and handling fee. I have enclosed my check or money order for $18, which includes the $3 shipping and handling fee. Please bill the credit card number below for $18.

___Send me both a subscription to PerformInk and "The Book: An Actor's Guide to Chicago" for a total of $38.95 ($27.95 for a subscription and a discounted subscriber price of $8 for "The Book," and a $3 shipping and handling fee) I have enclosed my check or money order for $38.95. Please bill the credit card number below for $38.95.

Visa/MasterCard/Discover #_____, Exp. _____

Order more copies of

The Book: An Actor's Guide to Chicago!

Give one to a friend!

Makes the perfect gift!

Name _____

Business Name _____

Address _____

City _____ St ____ Zip _____

Phone _____

Fax _____

e-mail _____

website _____

___Send me a copy of the 1998 edition of "The Book: An Actor's Guide to Chicago" for $15 plus a $3 shipping and handling fee. I have enclosed my check or money order for $18, which includes the $3 shipping and handling fee. Please bill the credit card number below for $18.

___Send me both a subscription to PerformInk and "The Book: An Actor's Guide to Chicago" for a total of $38.95 ($27.95 for a subscription and a discounted subscriber price of $8 for "The Book," and a $3 shipping and handling fee) I have enclosed my check or money order for $38.95. Please bill the credit card number below for $38.95.

Visa/MasterCard/Discover # _____, Exp. _____